Outdoor Living Projects

Outdoor Living Projects

JOHN BOWLER AND FRANK GARDNER

MURDOCH
B O O K S

CONTENTS

BUILDING BARBECUES 166

Garden furniture

Making outdoor furniture

Building outdoor furniture requires the same skills and tools as any other carpentry job, and as always a little forward planning will make the work much easier. Careful choice of materials will also result in a beautiful and long-lasting piece.

SUITING YOUR GARDEN

Before you begin work, spend some time deciding exactly what sort of garden furniture you need. Do you need a table for food or drinks as well as seats? Is your garden very small so that folding furniture is most suitable? Do you want furniture that is easily moved around the garden?

There is nothing worse than having your garden full of beautiful furniture you never use, so plan your requirements carefully.

CHOOSING MATERIALS

Outdoor furniture, by its very nature, is subjected to the weather and the materials you use must be able to withstand the elements if the item is to remain in good condition.

Suitable timbers include treated pine, Western red cedar and iroko. The latter two are much more expensive than pine, but can be worth the expense as they are very attractive. All timbers used outdoors require a protective finish, and the finish you choose will also affect your choice of timber. For instance, using iroko would be a waste if you are planning to paint the item, but if you are planning to use a clear oil finish

to achieve a natural look, it might be worth the expense.

The nails, screws and bolts you use for outdoor furniture should always be galvanized so that they don't rust.

WORK AREA

• A specific workshop area isn't a necessity for building any of the projects in this book. However, some pieces are quite large and you will need enough space for storing

Treated pine was used for this setting as it was to receive a painted finish.

materials and for moving easily around the project during the construction. An undercover area such as a garage might suffice, but if you don't have a fixed roof to work under, make sure you can keep the timber dry and clear of the ground while it is stored.

• Good lighting is a necessity, not only for comfort, but also for safety. Fluorescent lights are the best choice because they cast a brighter light with less shadow. Take care where you position your lights so you are not working in your own shadow and the light isn't in your eyes.

• Adhesives and paints can give off dangerous fumes, so always work in a well-ventilated area. Open windows and doors when applying adhesives or finishing coats.

• While an old table may be strong enough to serve as a workbench for small items, you will need a strong bench for most of these projects.

EQUIPMENT

Most of these projects can be completed using basic hand tools, but portable power tools will make the job easier and faster. A circular saw, electric drill, jigsaw and router are the most commonly used power tools in the home workshop.

SAFETY PRECAUTIONS

When using any type of portable power tool, make sure you are wearing the right safety gear. Always wear safety glasses that completely enclose the eyes and a dust mask (the

Outdoor furniture such as this arbour seat turns a garden into living space.

cartridge type is recommended if you have any respiratory problems). If you have long hair, tying it back is not enough protection – a cap or hairnet is essential. Also consider what clothing you will wear. Loose-fitting garments are dangerous when working with machinery.

BEFORE YOU START

Read right through the entire instructions before you begin a project. Check that you have the right tools, timber and hardware specified. If you are not familiar with a particular technique then try practising on a scrap of timber.

Barbecue table and bench

This sturdy outdoor setting is simple to make. The construction requires the minimum number of joints and is suitable for the less experienced woodworker.

MAKING THE TABLE TOP

1 Using a power mitre saw, cut two side rails and two end rails to length.

2 Use a router to cut a 20 x 20 mm rebate along one edge of each end rail. Measure in 70 mm from each end and square a line across the rebated side and edge. Set a marking gauge to 20 mm (the width of the rebate), turn over the rail and, working from the rebated edge, mark a line from the end to the 70 mm line. This part will be removed to create a flat section for the dowelled joint. Use a tenon saw to cut across the rebate and then a jigsaw to cut along the line. Round over the edge with abrasive paper.

3 Mark the dowel set-out on each end of the side rails (see the diagram at right). Use a 10 mm dowelling bit in an electric drill and bore the holes 26 mm deep. Place dowel centres in the holes and position the end rails at right angles to the side rails to mark the corresponding holes. Drill these holes 26 mm deep. Place adhesive in the holes and on the end of the rails. Insert the dowels and place the frame in sash cramps. Use scrap timber between cramps and frame to protect

TOOLS

- Rule or tape and pencil
- Jigsaw and tenon saw
- Power mitre saw
- Router with 20 mm straight bit
- Marking gauge
- Electric drill
- Drill bits: 3 mm and 4.5 mm twist bit, 10 mm dowelling bit
- 10 mm dowel centres
- Sash cramps
- Screwdriver to suit
- Sliding bevel
- Combination square
- Builders square
- Hammer
- Chisel: 25 mm

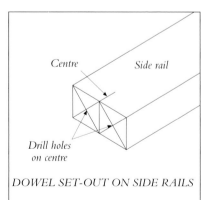

Centre *Side rail*

Drill holes on centre

DOWEL SET-OUT ON SIDE RAILS

A blue-on-white distressed finish gives this bench and table combo a contemporary look. It's perfect for dining al fresco with friends and family.

MATERIALS★

PART	MATERIAL	FINISHED LENGTH	NO.
Table			
Side rail	70 x 35 mm treated pine	1360 mm	2
End rail	90 x 35 mm treated pine	900 mm	2
Slat	70 x 20 mm treated pine	1360 mm	11
Cleat	70 x 35 mm treated pine	760 mm	3
Stretcher rail	70 x 35 mm treated pine	600 mm	2
Brace	70 x 35 mm treated pine	600 mm	2
Leg	70 x 35 mm treated pine	730 mm	4
Bench			
Leg	70 x 35 mm treated pine	580 mm	4
Bearer	70 x 35 mm treated pine	450 mm	2
Back upright	70 x 35 mm treated pine	630 mm	2
Arm	70 x 35 mm treated pine	550 mm	2
Back slat (top)	90 x 20 mm treated pine	1350 mm	1
Back slat	70 x 20 mm treated pine	1350 mm	2
Seat slat	70 x 20 mm treated pine	1350 mm	1
Seat slat (front)	70 x 20 mm treated pine	1330 mm	5
Stiffener	70 x 35 mm treated pine	1260 mm	1
Rail	40 x 20 mm treated pine	450 mm	1
Cleat	25 x 25 mm treated pine	450 mm	2

OTHER: Epoxy adhesive; abrasive paper: two sheets of 120 grit; eight 50 mm long 10 mm diameter timber dowels; 30 mm x 8 gauge galvanised countersunk screws; 40 mm x 8 gauge galvanised countersunk screws; 50 mm x 8 gauge galvanised countersunk screws; 65 mm x 8 gauge galvanised countersunk screws; 50 x 2.5 mm galvanised decking nails; preservative; finish of choice

★ Finished size: table 1500 mm long x 900 mm wide x 750 mm high; bench 1400 mm wide x 600 mm deep x 840 mm high.

the surface. Tighten the cramps and remove excess adhesive. Measure the diagonals for square. Leave to dry.

4 Cut eleven 1360 mm long slats and round over the ends and edges on the top surface with 120 grit abrasive

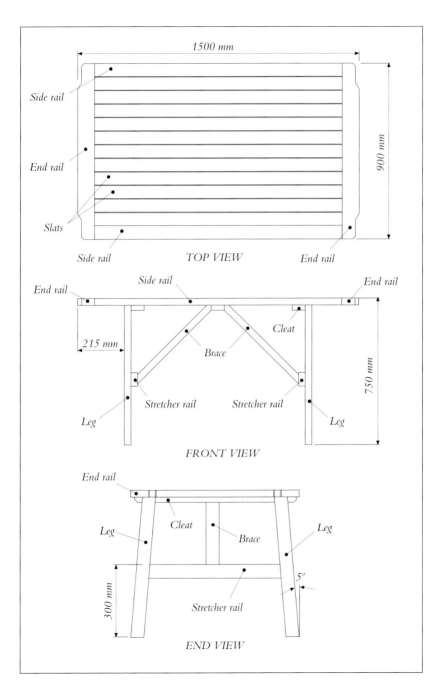

1500 mm

900 mm

Side rail

End rail

Slats

Side rail

TOP VIEW

End rail

End rail

Side rail

End rail

215 mm

Cleat

Brace

750 mm

Stretcher rail

Stretcher rail

Leg

Leg

FRONT VIEW

End rail

Leg

Cleat

Brace

Leg

300 mm

5°

Stretcher rail

END VIEW

paper. Lay the slats out upside down and fit the frame over the slats, allowing a gap of 3–5 mm between each board (a nail placed between the boards makes a useful spacer). For each slat drill one or two 4.5 mm clearance holes through the end rail, then 3 mm pilot holes into the underside of the slats. Hold each slat in position and fix from beneath with 30 mm x 8 gauge countersunk screws.

5 Using the end rail diagram to the right as a guide, make a cardboard template to shape each end rail. Draw the shape on to the rails in pencil. Cut the shape with a jigsaw. Clean the edge and round over with 120 grit abrasive paper.

6 Turn the top upside down and measure in 250 mm from each end. Square this mark across the bottom of the slats. Cut two 70 x 35 mm cleats to fit between the side rails. Bevel-cut the ends to 15 mm thick; round the edges over. Position the cleats on the inside of the marked lines and drill a 4.5 mm clearance hole followed by a 3 mm pilot hole

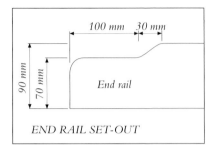

END RAIL SET-OUT

into each slat. Screw the cleats to each slat with a 40 mm x 8 gauge countersunk screw. Fix a third cleat across the centre of the slats. Skew a 50 mm galvanized screw into the side rails from each side of the cleats.

ADDING THE TABLE LEGS
7 The legs are cut with a 5 degree parallel bevel on each end. Set the angle on a mitre saw; or you can set a sliding bevel or create a pitch board (see the diagram opposite). To minimise waste, cut the legs from one length of timber. Bevel-cut one end at 5 degrees. Measure 730 mm, mark and cut parallel to the first cut. Mark and cut the other legs. The angle on the waste side is the same angle required for the next leg.

8 Cut two stretcher rails 600 mm long with 5 degree bevels (angled in opposite directions, not parallel as for the legs) at each end. Measure up 300 mm from the bottom of each leg and square a line across the outside edge. Place the legs flat with the spreader rail on top. Line up the top edge of the rail with the squared lines. Keep the ends flush with the

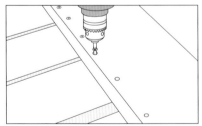

4 Fit the frame over the slats and fix in place with two 30 mm x 8 gauge countersunk screws into each slat.

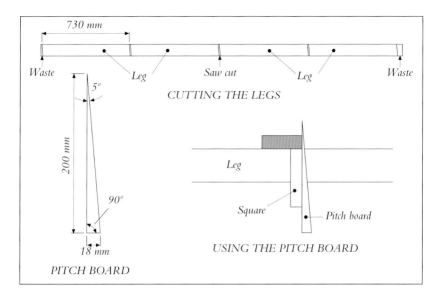

730 mm

Waste

Leg

Saw cut

Leg

Waste

5°

200 mm

90°

18 mm

PITCH BOARD

CUTTING THE LEGS

Leg

Square

Pitch board

USING THE PITCH BOARD

outside edge of the legs. Fix in position with two 50 mm x 8 gauge countersunk screws on each leg. Use the pitch board or sliding bevel to ensure the rail is at the correct angle.

9 Stand the assembled leg frame upside down against the outside edge of an end cleat. Centre it against the cleat. Fix each leg with two 65 mm x 8 gauge screws into the edge of the cleat. Repeat at the other end for the other leg frame.

10 To stabilize the table, cut a brace for each leg. Measure from the lower edge of the stretcher rail to the centre cleat. Cut two braces to this length. Fix them with two 50 mm x 8 gauge screws into the centre of the cleat and to the stretcher. Turn the table right side up and lightly sand with 120 grit abrasive paper.

CUTTING BENCH PIECES
11 Cut the four legs 580 mm long. Bevel both ends of each at 5 degrees. Cut two bearers 450 mm long.

12 Cut an 80 degree angle on one end of each bearer. Measure and mark 70 mm in from the opposite end of the bearer and square a line across the top edge (see the diagram on page 16). Square a second line across the same end 10 mm down from

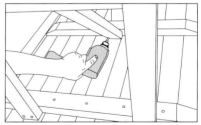

10 To stabilise the table, fix a brace from the lower edge of each stretcher to the centre cleat under the table top.

the top. Join these points on the face and cut the bevel. On the lower edge cut a 45 degree bevel. Cut two 630 mm back uprights, bevelling the top of each as for the bearers.

13 The arms fit around the back uprights and sit on top of the legs. Square-cut one end of an arm. Measure 70 mm from the end and, with a square and pencil, mark a line from the inside edge across the face.

14 Place a bearer on the edge of the arm and use it as a template to mark an 80 degree angle. Square the bevelled mark across the bottom of the arm. Use a gauge to mark 35 mm from the line to the squared end on each face. Remove this corner with a saw by cutting on the waste side of the line. Make the second arm in the same way, but so you have one left and one right arm. Round the ends of the arms with abrasive paper.

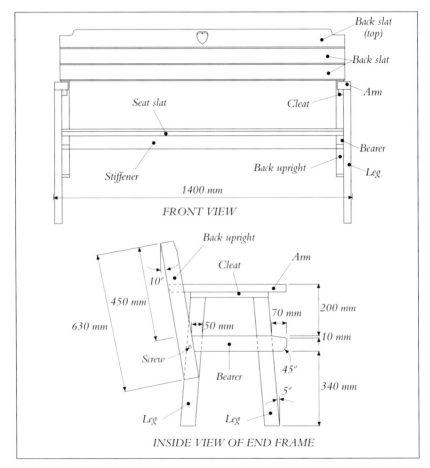

FRONT VIEW

INSIDE VIEW OF END FRAME

15 Cut the back slats. Shape the ends of the top slat with a jigsaw to match the table top. Round the edges with abrasive paper. Cut a design in the centre of the top slat.

ASSEMBLING THE BENCH

16 Square a line 10 mm in from both ends across the back of the back slats. Position the top slat on the bevelled end of one back upright. Line up the squared line with the outside face of the upright and fix with adhesive and two decking nails. Check for square with a builders square. Fix the other end of the slat to the other upright. Nail the other two back slats in place with a 10 mm overhang and a 4 mm gap between each. Cut two cleats from offcuts, turn the frame over and fix them across the back of the slats, 10 mm from the top (see the photograph on page 11).

17 Cut the seat slats. The long slat goes at the front and overhangs the bearers 10 mm each end; the others sit flush on the bearers. Fix them in place as for the back slats. Turn the seat over and cut the stiffener. It fits between the bearers, in line with the second slat. Fix it through the bearers with two 65 mm x 8 gauge screws at each end. Fix a 40 x 20 mm rail across the centre of the slats.

18 Measure up 340 mm from the bottom of each leg on the inside face and mark a line across the face of the leg, parallel to the end. Position each leg against the bearer, lining up the

This simply constructed bench is given an individual touch with a cut-out design in the top slat.

set-out with the bottom edge. The front legs sit against the edge of the front slat. The back legs are fixed 50 mm in from the bevelled end (see diagram opposite) and secured with two 50 mm x 8 gauge screws.

19 The back is positioned so its top is 450 mm above the top of the bearer. Hold the upright against the end of the bearer and fix it in place with two 50 mm screws into the leg.

20 Cut two 450 mm cleats to fit against the inside of the legs at the top. Cut the ends at a 5 degree angle to match the outside of the legs. Fix in place, flush on top and ends, with two 50 mm screws into each leg.

21 Place the arm on top of the legs, against the back. Fix with 50 mm screws through the upright and cleat. Sand the bench and apply a finish to match the table.

You can follow the sun or the shade all day with this clever seating arrangement constructed in treated pine and finished with paint designed for exterior use.

Circular seat

This circular seat is made in eight separate sections that can be joined to surround a tree trunk or other garden feature. Four sections make a semicircle that can stand against a wall.

CONSTRUCTING THE FRAME

1 Cut sixteen front legs and sixteen back legs to length. Use a power mitre saw to ensure an accurate square cut. Measure 70 mm from the top of each front leg and square a line across the face and down each edge. Set the marking gauge to 17.5 mm and mark across the end and down each edge to the 70 mm mark to indicate the halving joint.

2 Place a front leg next to a back leg with the bottom ends flush. Transfer the set-out lines from the front leg on to the back leg to mark a corresponding joint. Mark a cross on the face between the set-out lines. Square the set-out lines across both edges and mark a depth of 17.5 mm between the lines. Repeat for the remaining legs. Adjust the depth of cut on the circular saw to 17.5 mm. Clamp each leg in turn on a set of sawhorses and cut the joints with the saw by lining up the notch in the base plate with the set-out line and cutting on the waste side. Place several intermediate cuts in the timber to help remove the waste. Chisel the waste from each joint, first removing the bulk of the timber by

TOOLS
- Tape or rule and pencil
- Handsaw
- Circular saw
- Power mitre saw
- Jigsaw
- Builders square
- Combination square
- Marking gauge
- Chisel: 25 mm
- Hammer
- Nail punch
- Electric drill
- Drill bit: 4.5 mm
- Screwdriver
- Sliding bevel
- Hand plane
- Sawhorses

striking the chisel with a hammer or mallet, leaving approximately 3 mm of timber in the bottom of each joint. Clean the joint by paring in from each side down to the gauge line. Use the square to check the bottom is flat and adjust if required.

3 Cut the side rails to length. To cut the halving joints, measure 70 mm from each end and square a line

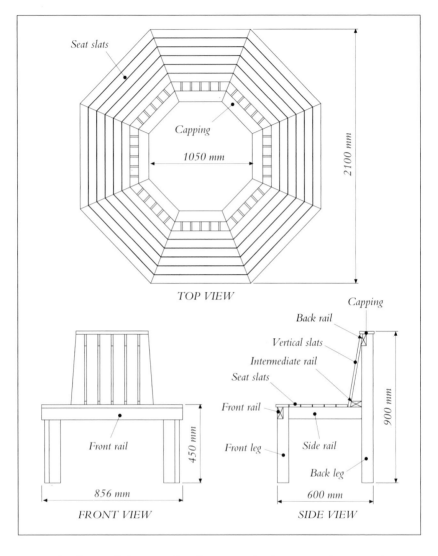

Seat slats

Capping

1050 mm

2100 mm

TOP VIEW

FRONT VIEW

Front rail

450 mm

856 mm

Capping

Back rail

Vertical slats

Intermediate rail

Seat slats

Front rail

Front leg

Side rail

Back leg

900 mm

600 mm

SIDE VIEW

across the face and down each side. Gauge the depth (17.5 mm); cut and remove the waste as before. Check each joint for accuracy of fit.

4 Place one front and one back leg on a flat surface with the recesses face up. Apply preservative to each joint. Place a side rail in the recesses; check the inside of the frame for square. Drill two 4.5 mm holes 20 mm across from the inside of the front joint with 3 mm pilot holes into the leg and secure with 30 mm x 8 gauge

MATERIALS★

PART	MATERIAL	FINISHED LENGTH	NO.
Front leg	70 x 35 mm treated pine	450 mm	16
Back leg	70 x 35 mm treated pine	875 mm	16
Side rail	70 x 35 mm treated pine	600 mm	16
Back rail	70 x 35 mm treated pine	462 mm	8
Front rail	70 x 35 mm treated pine	856 mm	8
Intermediate rail	70 x 35 mm treated pine	520 mm	8
Vertical slat (side)	90 x 20 mm treated pine★★	450 mm	16
Vertical slat (intermediate)	70 x 20 mm treated pine★★	450 mm	32
Seat slat	70 x 20 mm treated pine★★	870 mm	48
Capping	90 x 20 mm treated pine	480 mm	8

OTHER: 40 x 2.5 mm galvanised twisted-shank decking nails; 30 mm x 8 gauge countersunk galvanised chipboard screws; 50 mm x 8 gauge countersunk galvanised chipboard screws; abrasive paper: 100 grit; preservative; finish

★ Finished size: 2100 mm diameter x 900 mm high.
★★ The seat and vertical slats are cut from treated pine decking.

galvanized chipboard screws through the rail into the leg. In the back leg place a screw 20 mm in from the front edge and the other 20 mm from the back edge. Check the frame for square. The side with screw heads will be the inside of the frame. Assemble the other legs and side rails, so that each seat section will have a left and right frame.

5 Cut the rails to length. To make housings for the front and back rails, measure 70 mm from the top of each leg and square a line across both faces and the front edge. Measure 35 mm from the front edge on the inside face and gauge a line from the top of

the leg to the squared lines. Set a sliding bevel to 22.5 degrees and mark a line on the top of each front leg (see the diagram on page 22). Hold the frame upright in a vice and cut down the line on the waste side with a handsaw. Rotate the frame

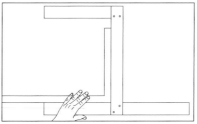

4 *Place one front leg, one back leg and one side rail on a flat surface. Check that the frame is square.*

90 degrees and cut the shoulders down to the first cut. Check for accuracy of fit and adjust as required.

6 The face of the back rail is bevelled to fit the vertical slats. Gauge a line 12 mm from the face along the top edge of the rail. Set the circular saw to cut at 10 degrees and use a rip fence to ensure a straight cut. Hold the timber firmly on edge in a vice and rip along the gauged line. Stand the rail on edge and cut the ends at 22.5 degrees using a power mitre saw. Apply a coat of preservative to the housings in the back legs and fix the rail flush on the outside face with two 50 mm x 8 gauge galvanized chipboard screws into the leg. The front rail is cut 856 mm long and is fixed in the same manner.

7 The intermediate rail will need one edge to be bevelled to allow the back to be sloped. Gauge a line 12 mm from the front edge along the face. Tilt the circular saw to 10 degrees and set the rip fence to 58 mm. Hold the rail firm in a vice or skew-nail it on a sawhorse. Cut

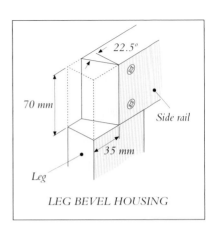

LEG BEVEL HOUSING

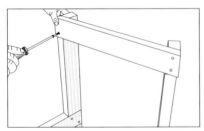

6 Fit the back rail with the bevelled edge on the outside face. Fix it with two screws into each leg.

the bevel along the length. Place the rail flat on the mitre saw and cut the ends at 22.5 degrees so they finish flush on the ends. Place them against the back legs and drill two holes at each end into the top of each side rail. Fix with 50 mm x 8 gauge galvanized chipboard screws.

ADDING THE SLATS

8 Cut the 90 x 20 mm vertical slats for the back. Position each slat over a side frame. Place a builders square on the top rail and square up the slat so that the outside edge is flush with the end of the intermediate rail. With a pencil, mark the back of the vertical slat, the end and top edge of the top rail. Remove the slat and place it face down on the sawhorses. Mark a line along the length of the slat between these two points. Set your circular saw to 22.5 degrees. Hold the slats firm and rip along the line on the waste side. Ensure that the saw cut bevels the correct way. Remember, the set-out line is on the back of the

slat, therefore the face is wider. You will require one left-hand and one right-hand slat for each section. Stand the slat on edge and cut the top of the marked length with a 10 degree bevel. Use a hand plane to round the edge on the front corner of the bevelled side. Apply some preservative to the rail and to the back of the slat. Fix the slat with two 40 x 2.5 mm twisted-shank nails.

9 Cut the remaining vertical slats to length with a 10 degree angle on top. Leave a gap of 10 mm between the slats. Fix as for the side slats.

10 The seat slats reduce in length from front to back. Select a straight slat to be cut for a starter board at the front of the seat. Cut one end at 22.5 degrees on the mitre saw. Position this slat with the bevelled end flush with the outside face of the frame. Allow 10 mm to overhang the front rail and mark the length on the underside at the opposite end frame. Turn the board over and cut to this set-out using the drop saw. Apply preservative, then fix the rail with two twisted-shank nails. As you are nailing close to the end, drill a pilot hole to prevent the timber splitting.

11 Cut one end of the next board. Position it on the seat, flush on the angled end. Use a 3 mm nail as a spacer between the boards at each end and mark the underside to determine the length. Cut and fix as for the starter board, ensuring the

The individual sections are screwed together to form a complete circle.

ends are flush with the outside of the end frames. Fix the remaining slats in the same way.

FINISHING

12 Apply a finish to each section of the project. If necessary, level the ground around the tree so the seat sits level and all sections line up with each other. Position each section in turn, joining them with 50 mm screws. Fix two screws into the front legs and three into the back legs, keeping the seat and backs aligned.

13 Cut the ends of the capping pieces at 22.5 degrees so that the shorter side fits on top of the back leg. Fix them with decking nails.

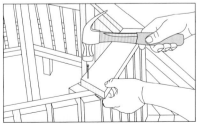

13 Cut the ends of the capping pieces at 22.5 degrees and fix them over the top of the back legs.

The ideal spot to while away your hard-earned leisure, this swing seat is constructed from treated pine and given a clear, natural finish.

Swing seat

The A-frame construction of this appealing garden swing takes up relatively little space, making it suitable for large or small gardens. It is not difficult to make.

MAKING THE FRAME

1 Cut the beam to length using a power mitre saw. Measure 150 mm from each end and square a line around the beam. This is the outside edge of the A-frame.

2 To mark the bevels at each end of the legs, set up a builders square with rafter buttons. Fix one button to the blade of the square at 316 mm and the other on the stock at 97 mm. Place the leg on edge and mark the position of the stock on the timber (see the diagram below). This is the bevel for the foot cut. Then mark the position of the blade on the edge of the timber. Slide the square along the timber, lining up the stock with the previous blade position. Mark the blade length again and slide the square along. Repeat until you have

TOOLS

- Tape or rule and pencil
- Power mitre saw
- Circular saw
- Jigsaw
- Handsaw
- Combination square
- Builders square and rafter buttons
- Sawhorses
- Hand plane
- Marking gauge
- Hammer
- Electric drill
- Drill bits: 4.5 mm, 8 mm, 10 mm
- Screwdriver and spanners
- G-cramps
- Chisel: 25 mm
- Cork sanding block

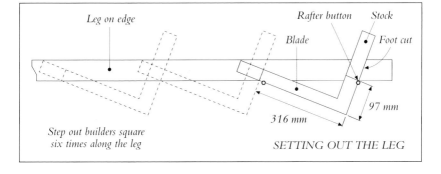

Leg on edge

Rafter button   Stock

Blade   Foot cut

Step out builders square
six times along the leg

316 mm   97 mm

SETTING OUT THE LEG

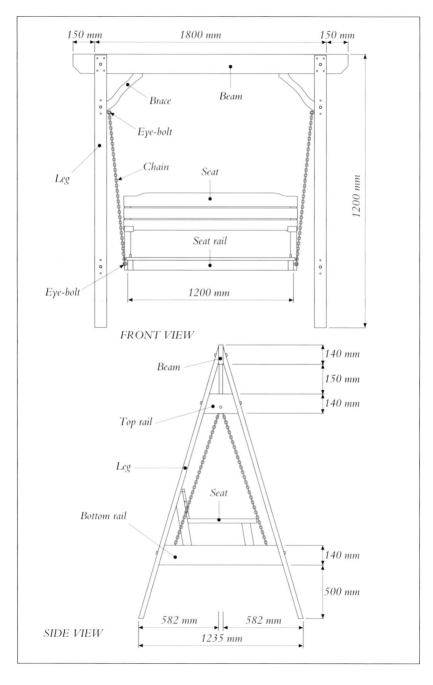

150 mm   1800 mm   150 mm

Brace

Beam

Eye-bolt

Leg

Chain

Seat

Seat rail

Eye-bolt

1200 mm

1200 mm

FRONT VIEW

140 mm

150 mm

140 mm

Beam

Top rail

Leg

Seat

Bottom rail

140 mm

500 mm

582 mm   582 mm

1235 mm

SIDE VIEW

MATERIALS★

PART	MATERIAL	FINISHED LENGTH	NO.
Frame			
Beam	140 x 45 mm treated pine	2100 mm	1
Leg	90 x 45 mm treated pine	1987 mm	4
Bottom rail	140 x 45 mm treated pine	960 mm	2
Top rail	140 x 45 mm treated pine	230 mm	2
Seat			
Bearer	70 x 35 mm treated pine	955 mm	2
Back upright	70 x 35 mm treated pine	600 mm	2
Seat rail	70 x 35 mm treated pine	1200 mm	2
Arm support	70 x 35 mm treated pine	275 mm	2
Arm	70 x 35 mm treated pine	600 mm	2
Seat slat	70 x 25 mm treated pine	1284 mm	8
Back slat	70 x 25 mm treated pine	1300 mm	2
Top slat	90 x 25 mm treated pine	1300 mm	1

OTHER: 65 mm x 8 gauge galvanised chipboard screws; twenty-four 50 mm x 8 gauge galvanised chipboard screws; 38 mm x 8 gauge galvanised chipboard screws; eight 75 mm x 10 gauge galvanised chipboard screws; 40 x 2.5 mm galvanised decking nails; 65 x 2.5 mm galvanised raised-head nails; eight 100 x 8 mm galvanised coach screws and washers; two 125 x 10 mm galvanised round-head bolts and nuts; abrasive paper: 120 grit; two 380 mm long wooden corner braces; six 100 mm galvanised eye-bolts with washers and lock nuts; six 5 mm galvanised snap hooks; 4.4 m of 20 mm galvanised chain; preservative; finish of choice

★ Finished size: 2100 mm wide x 1235 deep and 1900 high.

stepped the length six times. The last blade mark is the cut to go against the beam. Square these positions down each face of the leg; cut on the waste side. This is the leg template.

3 Clamp the timber on edge to the sawhorses and cut with a handsaw.

Follow the set-out lines and regularly check both sides of the cut, especially the top cut. If necessary, plane the cut end to even the bevel. To cut the second leg, place the first leg on top of it, edge to edge, and trace the bevels and length from the first leg on to the second leg. Cut to match.

4 Place the two legs on edge with the top ends resting either side of an offcut of beam timber. Move the bottom of the legs 1200 mm apart. Check that the top fits neatly against the offcut, and lay a straight edge against the feet to check the bevel. Adjust as required.

5 Measure 500 mm from the straight edge at the bottom of the legs and place a bottom rail over the legs. On the rail, mark the angle of the legs. On the legs, mark the top and bottom of the rail. Place a top rail across the legs, 150 mm down from the beam, parallel to the first rail. Mark as before. Remove the rails and join the set-out across the face. Cut the rails to length.

6 Check the fit. Use a square to transfer the marks down the inside face of the legs. Use these four pieces as a pattern for the other side frame. Construct it in the same way.

7 Set a gauge to 22 mm and mark a line on the inside face of each leg between the squared lines. Hold each

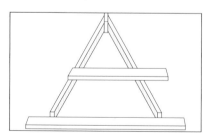

4 Check the fit of the legs against the beam. Place the bottom rail parallel to the bottom edge and mark the angle.

rail on the gauged line, between the squared lines. Nail a 65 x 2.5 mm raised-head nail through the outside of the leg. When all the joints are fitted and the frame has been nailed, drill through the leg with an 8 mm bit down to the centre of the end of each rail. Drill a 4.5 mm pilot hole as deep as possible into the end of the rails. Put a 100 x 8 mm coach screw with washer into the hole and tighten. Repeat at the ends of all rails.

8 Place the frame on the face of one leg. Slide the beam in place at the top of the frame. Line up the outer edge of the frame with the square marks on the beam. Drill a 10 mm hole through the leg, the beam and the other leg. Fix with a 125 x 10 mm round-head nut and bolt. Check the beam is square to the leg. Measure 30 mm up from the bottom of the beam and drill two 4.5 mm holes through the leg. Screw 65 mm screws through the leg, into the beam. Drill two 4.5 mm holes through the leg 30 mm from the top of the beam. Fix with 38 mm screws.

9 Fit the brace between the top rail and the beam. Fix the brace through the rail with a 65 mm screw. To fix the top of the brace to the bottom edge of the beam, drill a 4.5 mm hole near the end of the brace and fit a 38 mm screw into the beam.

CONSTRUCTING THE SEAT

10 Cut two bearers to length using the mitre saw. Square a line across the

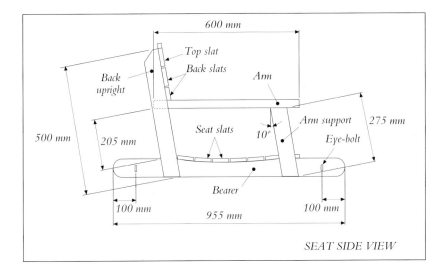

600 mm

Top slat

Back slats

Arm

Back upright

Seat slats

10°

Arm support

275 mm

Eye-bolt

500 mm

205 mm

Bearer

100 mm

955 mm

100 mm

SEAT SIDE VIEW

top edge, 200 mm from each end. Measure in another 70 mm and square a line as before (see the diagram on page 31). Mark the centre of the bearer and square a line across the top edge and down the faces. Mark 10 mm down the centre line and tack in a small nail. To curve the seat, bend a thin piece of timber over the nail and out to the 70 mm lines. Trace the curve on to the bearer. Clamp the bearer to a sawhorse and cut the curve on the waste side with a jigsaw. Smooth with abrasive paper.

11 Square both 200 mm set-out lines across the inside face and both edges of the bearers. Measure in 35 mm from this and square a line around all sides. Set a gauge to 10 mm and mark both edges between the lines for the rail housings. Clamp the bearers to a sawhorse and cut on the waste side. Clean the joint.

12 Cut two back uprights to length with one end 10 degrees off square. For the halving joint, measure in 72 mm and mark a shoulder line across the face, parallel to the angle cut. Square this line down each edge. Set a marking gauge to 17 mm and mark a line along the edges of the timber and across the end. Make left and right uprights. Clamp the upright flat on a sawhorse and cut the housing on the waste side. Make several cuts across the joint. Remove the waste; level the housing bottom.

13 Cut two arm supports, each end angled at 10 degrees. Set out and cut a housing at the bottom end as for the back uprights (see the diagram above). Cut one left and one right. Cut two seat rails 1200 mm long on the mitre saw. Apply preservative to the housing and the end of the rails. Position the rails in the housing on

the side of the bearers. Drill two 4.5 mm holes through the outside of the bearer. Fix the rails with 75 mm x 10 gauge screws. Fix the back uprights and arm supports to the bearers with three 50 mm x 8 gauge screws at the 200 mm set-out lines.

14 Cut two arms. Measure in 70 mm on one end and square a line across the face. Mark a line on the inside edge 10 degrees off square and square a line back across the bottom. Gauge a line 35 mm in from the edge, from the squared line on the face across the end and back to the squared line on the opposite face. Cut out the corner with a handsaw. Round the front end of the arm with a jigsaw. Smooth with 120 grit abrasive paper. To fix the arm, measure 205 mm from the top of the bearer up the back upright. Hold the arm on top of this mark and drill a 4.5 mm hole. Fit two 50 mm x 8 gauge galvanized chipboard screws through the back upright into the centre of the arm. Place another two screws through the top of the arm into the arm support.

ADDING THE SLATS

15 Cut eight seat slats with the mitre saw. The two front slats fit around the arm support. Hold the first slat with the ends flush on the outside face of the arm supports. Mark the position of the inside face of the support on the edge of the slat. Square this line across the face of the slat. The slat overhangs the seat rail by 20 mm. Set a gauge to 20 mm to mark a line parallel to the front edge, from the squared line to the outside edge. Place a cross on the opposite side of the line to indicate the section to be removed. Hold the slat on a sawhorse and, with a handsaw, rip down the grain to the squared line then across the slat on the waste side. Clean the cut with a chisel. Sand the sharp edge with 120 grit abrasive paper and apply preservative to the ends and underneath.

16 Fix the slat to the bearer with two 40 x 2.5 mm decking nails at each end. Evenly space two more nails into the rail. Fit the second slat with a 15 mm cut-out in the front edge to fit the back of the support.

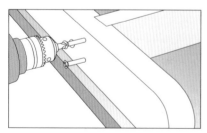

13 Fit the rails in the housings on the side of the bearers and fix them with two 75 mm screws.

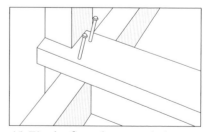

15 Fit the first slat around the arm support so that it overhangs the seat rail by 20 mm.

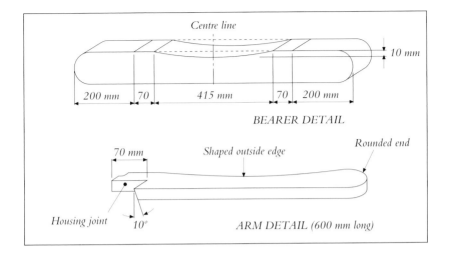

Centre line

10 mm

200 mm | *70* | *415 mm* | *70* | *200 mm*

BEARER DETAIL

70 mm

Shaped outside edge

Rounded end

Housing joint | *10°*

ARM DETAIL (600 mm long)

Leave a 5 mm gap between the slats. Nail the other slats to the bearers, overhanging 17 mm each end and with 5 mm between. Set out and cut the last seat slats to fit the upright.

17 Cut the top slat to length. Square a line 100 mm from each end. Gauge a line 70 mm in from the edge to the squared line. Use a can or jar to draw an inside and outside curve. Cut on the jigsaw. Place the slat on the back uprights, overhanging the top and ends by 5 mm. Fix with 40 x 2.5 mm decking nails. Cut and fix the second and third slats with a 5 mm gap between. Fit the third slat around the arms as before.

FINISHING

18 On the bearers measure 35 mm from the top edge and 100 mm from each end. Drill an 8 mm hole through the bearer and place a 100 mm eye-bolt through each hole.

Secure it with a washer and lock nut, with the eye square to the bearer. On the frame measure 100 mm up from the bottom of the top rail and drill an 8 mm hole through rail and brace. Place a 100 mm eye-bolt through the hole and secure it with washer and lock nut. Cut four 1100 mm lengths of chain. Attach the chain to the eye-bolts with a 5 mm snap hook.

19 Apply a suitable outdoor finish of your choice to the project to protect the timber from the weather.

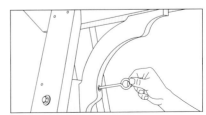

18 Drill a hole through both the brace and rail. Insert an eye-bolt and secure with a washer and nut.

Arbour seat

The lattice sides and roof of this sturdy arbour seat provide shelter from the sun while still letting through breezes to keep you cool. The construction is straightforward and does not require special skill.

PREPARING THE POSTS AND RAILS

1 Cut the four corner posts to length with a circular saw. Place the posts side by side with the ends flush and measure 350 mm from the bottom, then a further 90 mm. Use a builders square to transfer these marks across all the posts. Mark a cross between the set-out lines to represent the housing for the bottom rails. Select two back posts and square the set-out on to a second side of each. Remember, you will need one left-hand and one right-hand post. For the side intermediate rail housing, measure up 1000 mm from the top of the bottom rail housing then a further 90 mm, square the lines and mark with a cross as before (see the top diagram on page 34). Set a gauge and mark a line 10 mm in from the edge between each shoulder line.

2 Clamp one back post firmly on the sawhorses. Set the circular saw to cut 10 mm deep. Line up the notch in the base plate of the saw with the squared lines and slowly cut a through housing (cutting on the waste side of the set-out). Make several other cuts in the housing to

TOOLS
• Tape measure and pencil
• Circular saw
• Handsaw
• Builders square
• Marking gauge
• Chisel: 25 mm
• Electric drill
• Drill bit: 4.5 mm
• Sash cramps
• Screwdriver
• Hammer
• Rafter buttons
• Sawhorses

make it easier to remove the waste timber, and clean the bottom of the housing with a 25 mm chisel. Take care not to go past the gauged lines. Use an offcut of rail material to check the bottom of each housing for flatness and width. Cut the remaining housings in the back posts in the same way, and then cut the housings in the front posts.

3 Cut the side bottom and intermediate rails and the back bottom rail to length.

An asset to any garden, this arbour seat is constructed in treated pine and then given a protective coating of clear decking oil for a long life of year-round use.

4 Cut two side top rails. To enable these two rails to overhang the posts, measure 150 mm and then a further 90 mm from each end, and square lines at these points across the face and approximately 10 mm down each edge. Gauge a line 10 mm deep and cut the housings for the post. Determine the front and back of the rail. Square the set-out lines of the rear housing across the inside edge and opposite face of each rail. Set a marking gauge to 30 mm and mark a line between these set-out lines and in the bottom of the housing (see the diagram below). You will need a left-hand and a right-hand rail. Hold the timber on edge and cut down the set-out lines of the housing with a handsaw to the gauge lines. Remove the waste as before.

5 Cut the back top rail to length. Square a line across the face and down each side 30 mm from each end. Set a marking gauge to 10 mm and mark a line from the squared line along the edge and across the end. Cut and clean the housings.

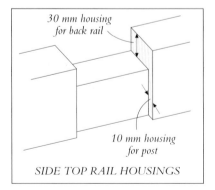

SIDE TOP RAIL HOUSINGS

30 mm housing for back rail

10 mm housing for post

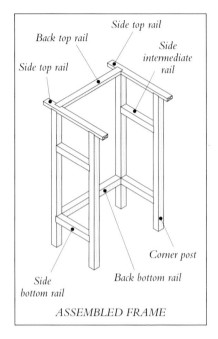

ASSEMBLED FRAME

Back top rail

Side top rail

Side top rail

Side intermediate rail

Corner post

Side bottom rail

Back bottom rail

ASSEMBLING THE FRAME

6 Apply preservative to all joints. Place the posts on a flat surface and position the side bottom rails one at a time in the housings with the outside faces flush. Drill two 4.5 mm holes at an angle through the bottom face of the rail. Hold the rail in the housing at 90 degrees to the post and fix it in place with two 65 mm screws. Additional screws placed through the top will add strength to the joint. Position the side intermediate rails and fix them as before. Take care to keep the frame as close as possible to square while you are assembling it. If you have sash cramps, place them over the frame to pull the joints tight. Place the top rail over the ends of the posts (ensure you have one left-hand

MATERIALS★

PART	MATERIAL	FINISHED LENGTH	NO.
Corner post	90 x 90 mm treated pine	2100 mm	4
Side rail	90 x 90 mm treated pine	620 mm	4
Back bottom rail	90 x 90 mm treated pine	1220 mm	1
Side top rail	90 x 45 mm treated pine	1080 mm	2
Back top rail	90 x 45 mm treated pine	1260 mm	1
Rafter	90 x 45 mm treated pine	925 mm	6
Trimmer	90 x 45 mm treated pine	423 mm	4
Seat trimmer	90 x 45 mm treated pine	480 mm	1
Seat front rail	90 x 35 mm treated pine	1200 mm	1
Seat centre upright	90 x 40 mm treated pine	700 mm	1
Seat back upright	40 x 40 mm treated pine	700 mm	2
Seat top rail	40 x 40 mm treated pine	1200 mm	1
Cleats	40 x 40 mm treated pine	to fit	2
Ridge	140 x 35 mm treated pine	1080 mm	1
Arch	140 x 45 mm treated pine	1200 mm	1
Seat/back slats	90 x 20 mm treated pine	1200 mm	12

OTHER: 65 mm x 8 gauge galvanised chipboard screws; 25 mm x 2 mm galvanised raised-head nails; 40 x 2.5 mm twisted-shank decking nails; two 75 mm nail plates; four metal joint connectors; lattice: one sheet 1800 x 1200 mm and one sheet 2400 x 1200 mm; about 50 m of 18 x 12 mm beading; abrasive paper: 80 grit; ready-made finial; preservative; finish of choice

★ Finished size: 1380 mm wide x 1080 mm deep x 2450 mm high.

and one right-hand frame) and drill four 4.5 mm holes through the face into the top of each post. Secure with 65 mm screws.

7 You may require a helping hand for the next step. Stand each side frame on its front edge and position the two back rails in the housings.

The top rail is screwed through the top face into the ends of the post with 65 mm screws. Fix a nail plate over the top of each joint. The bottom rail has four screws skewed into the post as before. If necessary, nail a temporary brace over the front side to keep the frame steady and parallel while you work.

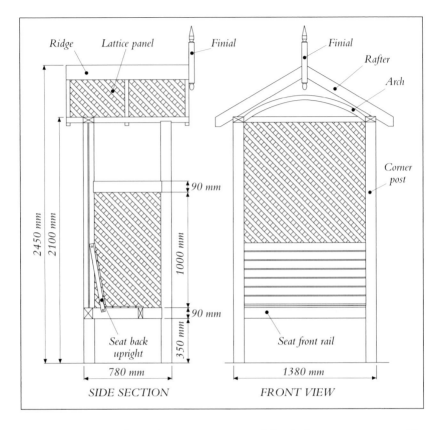

Ridge   Lattice panel   Finial   Finial   Rafter   Arch

2450 mm   2100 mm   90 mm   1000 mm   90 mm   350 mm

Corner post

Seat back upright

Seat front rail

780 mm   1380 mm

SIDE SECTION   FRONT VIEW

ADDING THE LATTICE

8 To determine the size of the lattice panel, measure the inside of the frame and reduce the measurement by 3 mm on all sides for clearance. Mark the required measurements on the face of the lattice and place a straight piece of timber on each mark. Draw a line the length of the cut along the straight edge. Place two 100 x 50 mm lengths of timber on a flat, firm surface. Position the lattice on top of the timber with the cutting line between the timbers. Nail or clamp the straight piece of timber on top of the lattice to serve as a guide for a circular saw. Check the blade will line up with the marked line and cut the lattice, taking care to keep the base plate against the straight edge and to support the offcut.

9 The lattice panels are beaded into the frame. Gauge a line 20 mm in from the back around the back opening. Cut the 18 x 12 mm bead to fit around all sides of the opening and fix it on the gauged line with 25 x 2 mm galvanized raised-head nails. Place the lattice in the frame

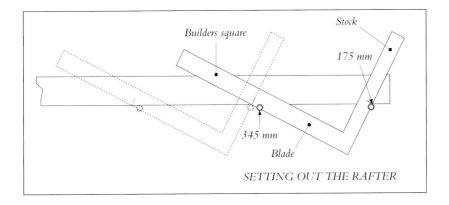

SETTING OUT THE RAFTER

and secure it in position by cutting and nailing another layer of beading around the opening on the other side of the lattice. Repeat the process for the side panels.

CONSTRUCTING THE ROOF

10 Set up a builders steel square with a pair of rafter buttons attached. Set the button on the blade to 345 mm (span) and that on the stock to 175 mm (rise). Place the square on a piece of rafter timber and pencil in the angle of the stock at the top (see the diagram above). Mark the position of the blade button. Slide the square along the rafter and line up the stock with the mark. Mark the blade button point for a second time and slide the square along once again to line up the stock with this point. Mark the line of the stock at this location. This line will represent the edge of the bird's-mouth housing. Measure 25 mm up this line and slide the square along the rafter to line the blade up with this mark

and mark the line of the blade. Measure out 150 mm along the blade from the line. Slide the square along the rafter and mark yet another line along the stock at the point. This is the bottom cut of the rafter.

11 The line for the top cut now needs to be repositioned by half the thickness of the ridge (17 mm) before it is cut. Position the square at the top of the rafter and slide down 17 mm. Cut the rafter to shape. Use a circular saw for each end and a handsaw for the bird's-mouth cuts. Take care with the cutting of this rafter, as it will be used as a template for all the rafters.

12 Place the template rafter on another piece of timber. Trace around the template and cut a second rafter to match. Place these two rafters in position with a piece of ridge material in between to test your set-out. Adjust as required. Place the template rafter on top of the other rafter material (three for each side).

Use a square to transfer the set-out on to the remaining rafters and cut as before.

13 Cut the ridge to the same length as the side top rails. Set a marking gauge to 20 mm and mark a line on the faces parallel to the top edge. Find the centre of the ridge. Place a rafter against the centre and mark the position, squaring the lines around to the opposite side. Place the ridge on one side top rail with the ends flush. Mark the front end so the set-out will be accurate. Transfer the centre rafter position on to the side rail. Repeat for the other side.

14 Place the first rafter on a flat surface. Stand the ridge on end and align the top edge of the rafter with the gauged line. Drill two 4.5 mm holes through the ridge. Fix the ridge to the end of the rafter with two 65 mm x 8 gauge screws. Fix the other rafters on this side to the ridge with two screws in each, ensuring they line up with the gauge line and the end one is flush with the ridge. Hold the opposite rafters in position

and drill a 4.5 mm hole through the top edge. A 65 mm x 8 gauge screw is used to fix each to the ridge. Drill another screw hole through the other side of the ridge at an angle to hold the lower edge of the rafter.

15 Lift the assembled roof frame into position. Check the outside rafters are flush on the ends and the centre rafter lines up with the previous set-out. Fix the frame in place through the top rails with 65 mm x 8 gauge screws. Cut a trimmer to fit between each rafter. Fix each trimmer with two screws, 30 mm from each end of the rafter and square to the top edge. Cut and bead in a lattice panel between each rafter in the same manner as for the sides and back.

FITTING THE SEAT

16 Cut two back uprights and one top rail for the seat. Square each end. Measure 100 mm from the back on the top of the side bottom rail and mark with a pencil on the inside edge. Hold the upright with the back edge on the 100 mm mark and the top end over the lattice beading on the corner post.

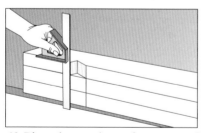

12 Place the template rafter on top of the other rafter material. Use a square to transfer the bird's-mouth set-out.

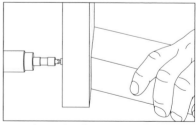

14 Place the first rafter on a flat surface. Stand the ridge on end and align the rafter with the gauged line.

Trace around the top on the beading. Cut the beading away with a sharp chisel so the upright sits flat against the post. Repeat on the other side. Fix the seat top rail to the top of each upright with the end flush, using one 65 mm x 8 gauge screw in each. Fix the assembled section in place with the top into the bead and the bottom aligned with the 100 mm mark.

17 Cut the seat front rail to length and fix it in place with a metal joint connector 480 mm in from the back posts. Cut a seat trimmer, fit it between the front and back rail, and secure it with screws. Add a joint connector to each end for extra strength. Fix the centre upright to the side of the trimmer and under the top rail. Cut two seat cleats to fit between the back upright and the front rail. Screw flush with the top edge of the side rail.

18 Cut twelve slats for the back and seat. Fix the back slats first with 40 x 2.5 mm twisted-shank nails, allowing a 3 mm gap between each board. Start at the bottom and work towards the

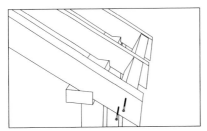

15 Fit a trimmer between each rafter. Check that the trimmers are square to the top edge, then fix in place.

top, keeping the ends flush with the uprights. Use two nails in each slat. Check periodically for parallel. Fix the seat slats in the same manner. The last board overhangs the front rail.

FINISHING

19 Measure the opening between the side top rails. Cut the piece of timber for the arch to fit between them. Square a line at the centre. On each end, measure up the thickness of the top side rails (45 mm) and tack a nail at this point. Tack another nail at the top of the centre line.

20 Bend a piece of beading around the three nails and trace on the inside of the curve. At the centre line measure down 45 mm and tack in another nail. Bend the beading around this nail and down to the bottom corners of the timber to make a parallel curve. Cut the curve on the waste side of the line with a jigsaw. Sand smooth with 80 grit abrasive paper.

21 Fix the arch in place with a 65 mm x 8 gauge screw through the bottom of the arch into the edge of the rail. A second screw should be skewed through the back to prevent the arch twisting around.

22 As a finishing touch, screw a ready-made finial to the top of the roof through the back of the rafters.

23 Complete the arbour seat by applying your chosen finish.

Designed on traditional lines to furnish your outdoor living area with style, this comfortable chair is constructed in sapele with a natural oil finish.

Traditional garden chair

This project for experienced woodworkers is sturdily constructed with mortise and tenon joints. The traditional styling suits any setting, and the seat is slightly curved for comfort.

CONSTRUCTING THE FRAME

1 Cut two back legs using a power mitre saw. Select and mark the face side and face edge. On one leg measure up 340 mm from one end and square a pencil mark across the face side and edge to represent the bottom of the side rail mortise (see the diagram on page 42). Mark the side rail height (66 mm) up from this and square a pencil line on the face side and edge. Set a mortise gauge to mark a 12 mm wide mortise 14 mm in from the face edge between these two set-out lines. Measure up a further 200 mm and then an additional 50 mm for the arm. Set out a mortise (12 x 50 mm) for the arm. Repeat this set-out for the second leg.

2 Cut two front legs. Select and mark the face side and face edge and cut the bottom end square. Place a back leg flat on the bench, face side up. Place a front leg on top, face side down, with the bottom ends and face edges flush. Use a square to transfer the side rail mortise position on to the face edge of the front leg. Use the mortise gauge to complete the set-out. Repeat for the other leg.

- Measuring tape and pencil
- Power mitre saw
- Jigsaw
- Tenon saw
- Mortise gauge
- Marking gauge
- Combination square
- Router with 3 mm rounding and 18 mm straight bit
- Electric drill
- Drill bits: 3 mm, 4.5 mm, 10 mm, countersink bits
- Two G-cramps
- Chisels: 12 mm mortise, 25 mm firmer
- Hand plane
- Builders square
- Hammer and nail punch
- Three sash cramps
- Screwdriver to suit

3 Using a pencil, mark the top of the back leg 200 mm above the arm mortise and square a line around the timber. Set a marking gauge to mark a line 66 mm from the front edge on the face side, and draw a line to the top of the side rail mortise. Draw a straight line from this intersection to

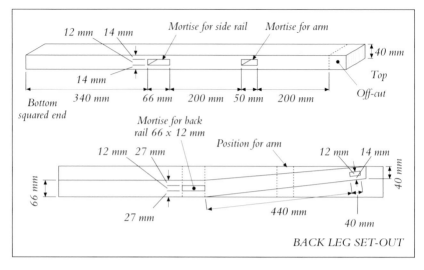

BACK LEG SET-OUT

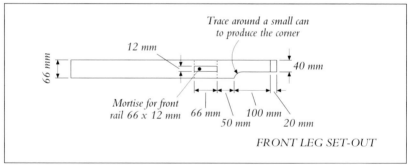

FRONT LEG SET-OUT

the square top line at the back edge of the timber. Measure and mark 40 mm in from the back edge at the top. Place a rule from the 40 mm mark to the top of the side rail mortise on the front edge of the timber. Mark with a pencil.

4 To remove the bulk of the waste from the mortises, use an electric drill with a 10 mm bit. Place masking tape around the bit to indicate the depth to be bored (40 mm). Hold the

timber over a solid point of the bench using a G–cramp or vice. Cut

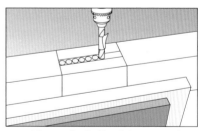

4 Drill out the bulk of the waste from the mortises, using masking tape on the bit to indicate the depth.

MATERIALS★

Part	Material	Finished length	No.
Back leg	90 x 40 mm sapele	900 mm	2
Front leg	66 x 40 mm sapele	580 mm	2
Side rail	66 x 40 mm sapele	510 mm	2
Front/back rail	66 x 40 mm sapele	560 mm	2
Top rail	66 x 30 mm sapele	560 mm	1
Arm	140 x 40 mm sapele	600 mm	2
Back slat	66 x 18 mm sapele	455 mm	4
Back slat (centre)	90 x 18 mm sapele	455 mm	1
Seat slat	66 x 18 mm sapele	600 mm	6
Seat slat (short)	66 x 18 mm sapele	520 mm	1
Cleat	35 x 20 mm sapele	484 mm	2

OTHER: 25 mm x 1.5 mm galvanised raised-head nails; 30 mm x 8 gauge galvanised countersunk screws; ten 50 mm x 8 gauge galvanised countersunk screws; abrasive paper: 120 grit; epoxy adhesive; preservative; finish of choice

★ All material sizes quoted are planed measurements. For timber types and sizes, see page 201. Finished size: 600 mm wide x 620 mm deep x 850 mm high.

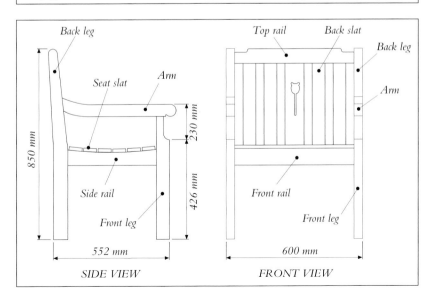

SIDE VIEW   FRONT VIEW

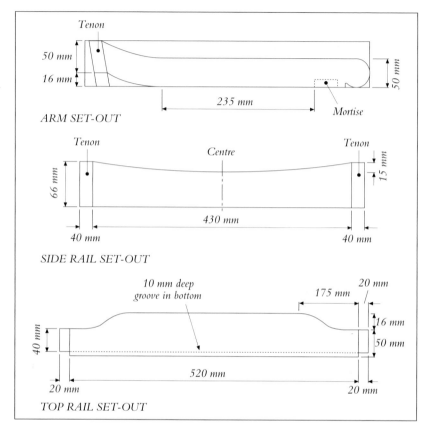

ARM SET-OUT

Tenon

50 mm

16 mm

235 mm

50 mm

Mortise

Tenon · Centre · Tenon

66 mm

15 mm

430 mm

40 mm · 40 mm

SIDE RAIL SET-OUT

10 mm deep
groove in bottom

175 mm

20 mm

16 mm

50 mm

40 mm

520 mm

20 mm · 20 mm

TOP RAIL SET-OUT

away the remaining waste with a 12 mm mortise chisel to finish 40 mm deep. Trim the mortise sides with a 25 mm firmer chisel. Take care chiselling out the mortise: hold the chisel upright so the recess is straight and true to size.

5 Clamp the back leg flat on a solid surface, with the cutting line on the face side overhanging the edge. Place the jigsaw on the surface and hold it firmly. Cut slowly along the line on the waste side. Take it easy, as the

timber is thick and the saw may jump. Use a new, sharp blade for the best result. Place the cut leg on edge

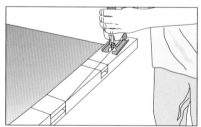

5 Shape the back leg by cutting along the set-out using a jigsaw held firmly to prevent it jumping.

44

in a vice and true up the edges with a hand plane. Check the face side is square. Round over the tops of the legs with abrasive paper.

6 For the top rail mortise, measure up the face edge of the back leg 440 mm from the back rail mortise. Then measure up 40 mm (the length of the mortise) and square a line across the face side at these points. Set the mortise gauge to mark a 12 mm wide mortise, 14 mm in from the front edge. Repeat for the other leg, remembering you need one left-hand and one right-hand leg. Drill and chisel the mortise 20 mm deep.

7 To shape the front legs, measure up 50 mm from the top of the side rails and square a pencil line around the leg. Measure 40 mm in from the back edge on this line. Pencil a parallel line from this mark to the top of the leg. With a small can or jar, trace a curve between the parallel line and the front edge of the leg. Cut the curve with a jigsaw. Clean up the edge with abrasive paper.

8 On the front leg measure 150 mm up from the top edge of the side rail mortise and square a shoulder line right around the leg. This will leave 20 mm above the line for a tenon. Set the mortise gauge as for the side rail (12 mm wide and 14 mm in from the edge) and mark from the shoulder line on the face edge, up across the end and down to the other shoulder line.

9 Hold the leg upright in a vice and, with a tenon saw, cut down both sides of the tenon on the waste side to the squared shoulder lines. Place the leg flat on the bench. Hold it firmly with a cramp or bench hook and cut across the shoulder lines to remove the waste.

10 Using the mitre saw, cut the side rails 510 mm long. Measure in 40 mm from each end and square a shoulder line all around the timber. Mark the tenons 12 mm wide out from these shoulders and around the end. Hold the rails upright in a vice and cut as before. Check for fit in the legs and adjust by paring a little at a time away from the face of the tenons. Take care to remove any waste from the correct side to ensure the faces remain flush.

MAKING THE ARMS

11 Position the legs on the side rail and secure with a sash cramp. Use a

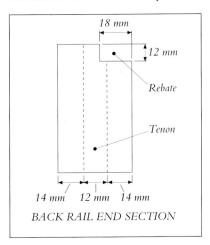

18 mm

12 mm

Rebate

Tenon

14 mm   12 mm   14 mm

BACK RAIL END SECTION

builders square to check each leg is square to the side rail. Cut the arms to length and hold one under the leg frame with the top edge in line with the top edge of the arm mortise in the back leg. Place the arm about 20 mm past the face edge of the back leg to allow the tenon to fit into the mortise in the back leg. The bottom edge should be in line with the shoulder of the front leg tenon. Trace around the tenon at the front and mark the shoulder line at the back. Square the tenon tracing around the bottom edge of the arm, and use the mortise gauge to set out the mortise. Drill out and cut the mortise 20 mm deep.

12 The tenon at the back of the arm has a bevelled shoulder to correspond to the slope on the back leg (see the diagram on page 43). Square the marked shoulder line across each edge with a pencil. Turn the arm over and use a rule to line up each squared line and mark the shoulder with a pencil. Use the mortise gauge to mark the tenon and cut it as before. Reposition the arm under the legs and mark the width of the tenon on the face side of the arm.

13 Place the arm flat on the bench. Measure 235 mm from the front mortise along the lower edge and mark across the face side and down the lower edge. Place a thin piece of timber from this point to the bottom of the tenon and mark the curved line with a pencil. Cut the curve with a jigsaw. Mark a parallel line

---

USING A ROUTER

- Read the manufacturer's instructions before operating.
- Always secure the work with cramps or a vice, leaving both hands free to operate the router.
- Wear safety glasses, hearing protection and a dust mask when operating the router.
- Use a scrap of timber to test the router setting before cutting into your project.

---

50 mm up from the lower edge to the squared line. Continue marking parallel to the curved line up to the top of the tenon. Round over and shape the front end of the arm with a jigsaw and abrasive paper.

14 The side rail has a slight curve in the top edge, 15 mm deep in the centre, sloping up to each end. Use a thin piece of timber and a pencil to shape the curve. Cut with a jigsaw.

15 Cut the three rails. Cut a 20 mm tenon either end of each rail, with 9 mm shoulders for the top rail and 14 mm for the front and back rails. To curve the upper edge of the top rail, fix nails 50 mm up from the lower edge and 175 mm in from each shoulder. Use a thin piece of timber and pencil to create the curve and cut along it with a jigsaw. Sand with 120 grit abrasive paper. Place a 3 mm pencil rounding bit in a router and run a small round along the top of

the rail. Rout a groove 10 mm deep and 18 mm wide in the lower edge for the back slats.

16 To reduce the top rail tenon from 50 mm to 40 mm, place an 18 mm straight bit in the router. Set the fence on the base so the cutter will run in the centre of the rail, 6 mm in from the edge. Hold the rail firmly upside down in a vice and run the router from left to right with the fence held against the face of the rail.

17 Place the back rail in the vice and adjust the router to cut a rebate in the top edge 12 mm deep and 18 mm wide. Check the fit of all the joints, adjusting as required. At the end of the tenons, cut a mitre with the long face towards the outside.

ASSEMBLING THE CHAIR

18 Assemble each side frame in sash cramps without adhesive. Place a scrap block between the job and the cramps to prevent marking the timber. Adjust it as necessary. Remove any marks by sanding with 120 grit abrasive paper.

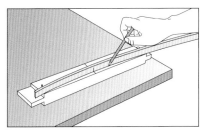

15 Place a piece of timber against the nails at the shoulders and 50 mm up from the centre, and draw the curve.

The centre slat can be decorated with your own cut-out design, or a ready-made baluster can be purchased.

19 Use a small brush or stick to apply epoxy adhesive to the joints, taking care to follow the directions provided. Coat the sides of the tenons and shoulder with theadhesive and smear a little around the inside of the mortise before bringing the joint together. Assemble the frame with two sash cramps underneath, closing up the side rail joint and the arm joint. Use another cramp over the top of the front leg to close the joint under the arm. Place a builders square on each leg and side rail to check for square. Adjust as required. Sight across the job to ensure there is no twist. If necessary, adjust the cramps to correct this. Additional weights or cramps placed on top of the frame can also help. Remove any excess adhesive. When the adhesive has dried, remove the frame from the cramps and use a hand plane to make the surface of the joints flush. Sand the face with 120 grit abrasive paper.

20 Check the remaining rails for fit, with the back rail rebate on the top inside edge. Once satisfied, apply the adhesive and place the sash cramps across the chair parallel to the rails. Lay a builders square inside the frame to check for square. Also check under the leg, between the front and back rails. Remove any excess adhesive. Once the adhesive has dried, remove the cramps and sand the frame to remove any adhesive or pencil marks.

FIXING THE SLATS

21 Cut four back slats to fit between the groove in the top rail and the rebate in the back rail. Cut a wider slat for the centre and cut out a design in the centre. Turn the chair over and position each slat. Maintain a 28 mm space between each slat. Hammer two 25 mm nails through the back of the slat into the top rail groove. Fix the slats into the back rail rebate with two screws measuring 30 mm.

22 Cut two cleats to fit between the front and back rails. Hold one in position against the inside of the side rail, and trace the curved shape of the side rail on to the face of the cleat. Cut the curve with a jigsaw and fix the cleat with four 30 mm screws. Repeat for the second cleat.

23 Cut the seat slats. Position them with the short slat between the front legs, to check the accuracy of the fit. The 600 mm slats overhang each side by 3 mm. Working from the back rail, fix them to the cleats from underneath with two 30 mm screws at each end. Use a nail to keep an even gap between each slat. Round over the front edge of the short slat. Position the front slat between the front legs and counter-bore from underneath the front rail. Fix with two 50 mm screws.

24 Strengthen the corners with scrap timber blocks approximately 150 mm long. Cut each end at 45 degrees to fit against the rail. Fix with a 50 mm screw at each end.

25 Sand out any marks and apply a protective finish so that the chair can be left outside if desired.

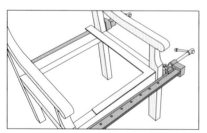

20 Assemble the chair frame, apply adhesive and fit sash cramps parallel to the rails. Check for square.

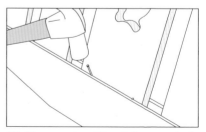

21 Hammer two 25 x 1.5 mm raised-head galvanised nails through the back of the slat into the top rail groove.

Tools for making garden furniture

Some of the most useful tools for making garden furniture are shown below. Build up your tool kit gradually – most of the tools can be purchased from your local hardware store.

SMOOTHING PLANE
Used to smooth the surface of timber before sanding

NAIL PUNCH
Small metal tool used with a hammer for driving a nail head below the surface

ELECTRIC DRILL
Power-driven drill with a variety of bits

CIRCULAR SAW
Power saw for making straight cuts through timber, masonry or metal

MEASURING TAPE
Spring-loaded, flexible steel blade marked in metric units of measure

JIGSAW Small electric saw with thin blade for cutting curves

G-CRAMP
Holds work firmly to a surface

SASH CRAMP Long adjustable cramp with screw tension at one end and adjustable sliding stop

BUILDERS SQUARE
Flat, right-angled device for determining 90 degree angles

SPIRIT LEVEL
Used to test work for level (horizontal) and plumb (vertical)

ROUTER Used for hollowing out or cutting grooves in timber

CLAW HAMMER
Hammer with a round head for driving nails and a split claw for removing them

CHISEL Used to cut grooves or housings in timber

Building decks

A deck provides a comfortable area for outdoor living, whether it is attached to the house or built in a sheltered corner of the garden.

Planning your deck

Careful planning and attention to the design before you start will make building your deck easier – and you'll end up with a deck that satisfies all your requirements.

WHY BUILD A DECK?

A deck extends your living area, providing a level area outside where you can sit comfortably. It is also practical as it will:
• compensate for sloping land;
• eliminate the problem of damp or shady areas where grass won't grow;
• increase the value of your house.

THE SIZE

The size of your deck will depend on the area available, its proposed function and, of course, your budget.

You may want to use the deck as:
• a place for children to play;
• an entertainment area;
• a place for outdoor barbecuing;
• a place to relax;
• a bridge or walkway;
• a surround for a pool, spa or children's sandpit.

A family of four to six people will generally need a deck approximately 12 m^2 to be comfortable. This will allow for a table and chairs but not a barbecue or plants. A safe estimate would be 2–2.5 m^2 per person.

THE LOCATION

The ideal location for a deck is on the southern side of the house where it will catch the summer sun. If this isn't possible, build it where it will be most useful. Note where shadows are cast on the ground as the sun moves through the sky from season to season. If necessary, add a screen or covered pergola to protect your deck from wind, rain or strong sun.

Other points to consider are:
• proximity to the house, especially the kitchen or family room;
• access to the garden;
• views;
• privacy (both your own and that of your neighbours).

TYPES OF DECKS

There are two main types of decks: attached and free-standing. An attached deck may be classified as a balcony or porch. It is fixed to the building for stability by means of a ledger, and so offers easy access to the house and its facilities.

A free-standing deck is an independent structure that supports itself. Instead of a ledger it has another row of posts. It is usually set away from the house but can be next to the house if you want to reduce the stress and load on the house and its footings. This type of deck is usually supported on brick piers or posts embedded in the ground. Posts supported in stirrups may be used, but these require additional bracing.

A free-standing deck can be built anywhere in the garden to take in a view, make better use of sloping land or surround a pool. It can be at ground level or raised, and it can be built in any shape, geometric or irregular. Walkways are essentially free-standing decks.

The basic elements of a deck are the same, whatever the type (see the diagram opposite).

DESIGNING A DECK

Once you have determined the function, size and location of your project, lay some timber around to mock up a full-size outline of the proposed deck. If you do not have timber available, use rope or even a garden hose to represent the outline.

Test out the area by positioning the tables, chairs or barbecue that will be used on the deck. Can you move around them comfortably? Will there be sufficient room to enjoy your deck? If not, you may need to increase the size or change the shape. However, keep in mind that bigger is not always better. Too big a deck could overpower the house and garden.

Be creative with your design, but keep it simple or it will be harder to build and will cost more. A split-level deck can make building on a steep site much easier, as it reduces the overall height of the construction. It also helps the deck to blend into the garden.

ACCESS

If you are attaching a deck to the house, consider how to ensure a smooth traffic flow from one to the other. Draw a plan of the rooms affected by the deck and map the traffic flow. You may need to move a door or replace a window with one (this should be done before the deck is built). A double-width door will allow the room inside to operate as an extension of the deck.

Decide whether you want stairs from the deck to the garden and where to locate them so they will provide a convenient entry.

ADDED FEATURES

Rocks or trees can be incorporated into the deck. Deciduous trees give shade in summer and let light in during winter. Allow room for the tree to grow and move with the wind. Lay temporary decking boards that can be removed as it grows.

Handrails and, perhaps, a pergola can be built as one with the deck by extending the posts up to the relevant height.

PREPARING PLANS

Once you have settled on a design, make some sketches of the deck with the dimensions on them. Before finalising the project, discuss these with your local Building Control office to check whether there are restrictions. You may need to provide larger scale plans (with construction details) and obtain development and building approval before starting.

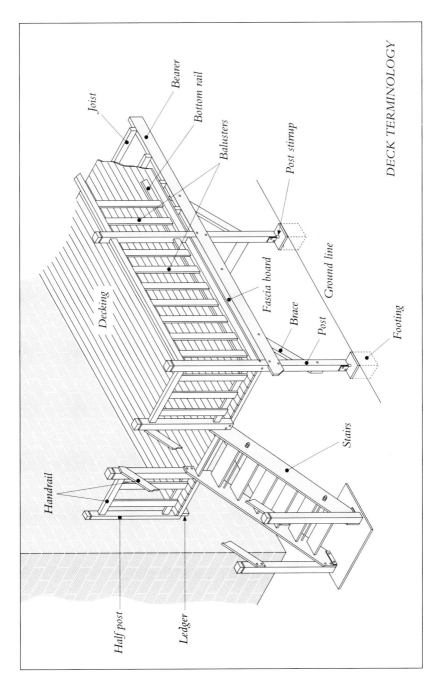

DECK TERMINOLOGY

Joist

Bearer

Bottom rail

Balusters

Post stirrup

Fascia board

Ground line

Brace

Post

Footing

Decking

Stairs

Handrail

Half post

Ledger

Choosing materials

Select the materials for your deck carefully, and it will last for many years. If the timbers and hardware are not strong enough, the deck may actually be dangerous.

CHOOSING THE RIGHT TIMBER

The timber used for a deck will be exposed to all types of weather conditions and must be able to withstand them. With the increase in the numbers of wood-boring insects, it must also resist their attacks.

If you use unseasoned timber it will inevitably shrink, warp or bow. Most hardwood is only semi-seasoned when purchased, as fully seasoned hardwood is very difficult to work. However, most treated timber is seasoned.

When buying timber for your project, watch for faults such as bowing or twisting. Lightly bowed or twisted timber may be flattened or pulled straight while it is fixed into position. Badly affected timber may be unusable.

DURABILITY

Hardwoods have a high durability and can be used both in and out of the ground. However, it is recommended that any timber in direct contact with the ground be treated with a suitable preservative.

Any timber used in the ground will require a higher level of protection than that being used above the ground. There are various standards of rating timber for durability against the elements and resistance to attack. Any hardwood placed in the ground must have a high durability rating. Low-rated timber should not be used for weather-exposed structural members such as posts, bearers, joists or decking unless it has been pressure-treated.

PRESSURE-TREATED TIMBER

The most commonly used timbers for decks are pressure-treated softwoods such as the many varieties of pine. Preservative-treated softwoods are readily available from most timber merchants and are commonly treated with a compound of copper, chromium and arsenic, known as CCA. This gives the timber a characteristic green tone.

When using timber treated with CCA, wear gloves and a dust mask while sawing. Any cut or sawn surface of this material will need to be re-sealed to ensure its effectiveness in resisting attack. Dispose of any offcuts by burying them – do not burn them, as the smoke and ash created are toxic.

Commercially treated softwoods are available. These can be bought with a range of hazard levels from a

Using good-quality timbers with the appropriate durability and stress gradings will ensure your deck is strong and lasts for many years.

EUROPEAN TREATED TIMBER HAZARD CLASSES

CLASS	USE
1	Internal, dry conditions only (borer-immunized) for furniture, panelling, framing and joinery
2	Internal conditions with risk of wetting for tiling battens (moderate borer and decay protection), timber in flat and pitched roofs, frame timbers and some joists
3	Exterior, weather-exposed, above-ground timber (moderate decay protection) for (3A) external joinery and cladding; (3B) fence rails and boards and gates
4	In contact with ground or fresh water, permanently exposed to wetting (full decay protection) for (4A) pergolas, fence posts, sleepers, poles and playground equipment; (4B) lock gates and revetment; (4C) cooling tower packing
5	Used specifically in marine conditions where floating on or immersed in salt water (marine borer and decay protection)

Information courtesy of the British Wood Preserving and Damp-proofing Association. Website: www.bwdpa.co.uk

TIMBER STRESS GRADINGS

SPECIES	AVAILABILITY	STRESS GRADING
Radiata pine, hoop pine and other plantation pines	Unseasoned	C16, C24
	Seasoned	C16, C24
Larch	Unseasoned	C16, C24
	Seasoned	C24
European whitewood	Unseasoned	C16, C24
	Seasoned	C16, C24
European redwood	Seasoned	C16, C24
Sitka spruce	Seasoned	C16
Fir	Seasoned	C16, C24

Ask your local timber merchants about available hardwoods and their uses.

This free-standing octagonal deck was built to cover an area below a large tree where grass would not grow. It is now a pleasant place to sit in summer.

low to a high level of treatment. Brush-on preservative should be applied to all sawn or shaped surfaces.

Some treated timber may be water-repellent, but it will still weather, turning silvery grey over time. A decking oil or stain will counteract this, although it will require some maintenance.

Always take precautions when using treated timber:

• Always wear gloves when handling treated timber.

• Use a dust mask and goggles when machining, sawing or sanding.

• Ensure there is good ventilation in the work area.

• Wash your hands and face before drinking or eating.

• Wash work clothes separately.

• Never use treated timber for heating or cooking, especially on barbecues.

STRESS GRADINGS

Timber is also stress-graded. The 'C' rating is followed by a number, which indicates the bending stress. The higher the number the greater the stress it can withstand. Normally, bearers and joists should not be any less than C24; posts may be hardwood, C24 or greater if seasoned softwood. In the tables on pages 98 and 100 'oak' is used as a shorthand for 'hardwood' for reasons of space.

SPECIFICATIONS FOR DECK TIMBERS

The timber sizes suggested for use in the various parts of the deck (see the tables on pages 61–3) are a rough guide only. Consult your local Building Control office for details of the specifications required in your local area. Note that the standards in England and Wales are different from those in Scotland.

HARDWARE

Any deck is only as good as its fasteners, so make sure you always use good-quality fittings and fasteners that will stand the test of time.

Most fasteners and fittings are made from mild steel with a protective coating and, in most situations, hot-dipped galvanising is the preferred coating. Stainless-steel fasteners may be needed where there are high-corrosive conditions, such as decks built around salt-water pools or those built in areas subject to sea spray. Other metals such as brass and copper may be appropriate in some conditions, depending on the preservative used – check with your hardware supplier.

Machine or roundhead bolts hold structural members together far more strongly than nails. Coach screws may be used where access is restricted to one side. Washers should be used on both ends of machine bolts and also under the head of coach screws to prevent them from pulling too far into the timber.

Masonry anchors may be required to fix ledgers to brick walls, or stirrups to footings. Use the appropriate size of anchor – if the anchor is too short the device may

POST SIZES FOR DECKS

| | | MAXIMUM HEIGHT★★ | |
| | | SPACING BETWEEN EACH POST | |
STRESS GRADE	POST SIZE★	1800 mm	3600 mm
C16 unseasoned softwood	100 x 100 mm	3000 mm	2000 mm
	125 x 125 mm	4500 mm	3200 mm
C24 seasoned softwood	100 mm diameter	1900 mm	1300 mm
	90 x 90 mm/125 mm diameter	2700 mm	1900 mm
	150 mm diameter	4800 mm	3400 mm
Hardwood or better seasoned softwood	70 x 70 mm/100 mm diameter	2400 mm	2400 mm
	90 x 90 mm/125 mm diameter	3000 mm	2400 mm
	150 mm diameter	4800 mm	3700 mm

★ When using sawn timber, increase the section size to the next largest, for example if using 90 x 90 mm, order 100 x 100 mm.
★★ Maximum height is taken from finished ground level.

DECK BEARER SIZES (SINGLE SPAN)

| | | SIZE OF BEARERS (mm) | | |
| | | MAXIMUM BEARER SPAN | | |
STRESS GRADE	JOIST SPAN	1800 mm	2400 mm	3000 mm
C16 seasoned softwood	1800 mm	120 x 70	170 x 70	240 x 70
	2400 mm	140 x 70	190 x 70	240 x 70
	3000 mm	170 x 70	240 x 70	
C20 seasoned softwood	1800 mm	120 x 70	170 x 70	190 x 70
	2400 mm	120 x 70	170 x 70	240 x 70
	3000 mm	140 x 70	190 x 70	240 x 70
C24 seasoned softwood	1800 mm	120 x 70	170 x 70	190 x 70
	2400 mm	120 x 70	170 x 70	240 x 70
	3000 mm	140 x 70	170 x 70	240 x 70
	3600 mm	140 x 70	190 x 70	240 x 70

MAXIMUM JOIST SPAN (AND CANTILEVER) WITH JOISTS AT 450 mm CENTRES (mm)			
UNSEASONED TIMBER	C16	C24	HARDWOOD
150 x 50 mm	2800 (800)	2900 (800)	3400 (900)
175 x 50 mm	3000 (800)	3600 (1000)	3900 (1100)
200 x 50 mm	3800 (1100)	4000 (1100)	4300 (1200)
225 x 50 mm	4200 (1200)	4300 (1200)	
250 x 50 mm	4500 (1300)	4700 (1400)	
275 x 50 mm	4900 (1400)	5100 (1500)	
SEASONED TIMBER	C16	C24	HARDWOOD
140 x 45 mm	2600 (700)	2600 (700)	3100 (900)
190 x 45 mm	3500 (900)	3700 (1000)	3900 (1100)

not hold tight; if it is too thin it may snap when subjected to stress.

The decking itself is subject to constant movement as it expands and contracts according to the weather, and as people walk over it. Galvanized nails with a spiral or twisted shank are best for fixing it, as lost-head (bullet-head) plain-shank nails do not have as much holding power. Lost-head nails are satisfactory for the framework.

There are special decking screws available with countersunk heads, but

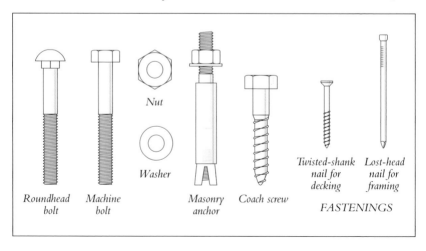

Nut

Washer

Roundhead bolt

Machine bolt

Masonry anchor

Coach screw

Twisted-shank nail for decking

Lost-head nail for framing

FASTENINGS

MAXIMUM JOIST SPAN (AND CANTILEVER) WITH JOISTS AT 600 mm CENTRES (mm)			
UNSEASONED TIMBER	C16	C24	HARDWOOD
150 x 50 mm	2700 (700)	2800 (800)	3100 (900)
175 x 50 mm	3200 (900)	3300 (1000)	3600 (1000)
200 x 50 mm	3600 (1000)	3700 (1000)	4000 (1100)
225 x 50 mm	3900 (1100)	4000 (1200)	
250 x 50 mm	4200 (1200)	4400 (1300)	
275 x 50 mm	4500 (1300)	4700 (1400)	
300 x 50 mm	4900 (1400)	5000 (1400)	
SEASONED TIMBER	C16	C24	HARDWOOD
140 x 45 mm	2500 (600)	2500 (700)	2900 (900)
190 x 45 mm	3200 (900)	3500 (1000)	3600 (1000)

they are only needed under extreme conditions. A well-nailed deck will normally give long service.

Other metal timber connectors, such as nail plates, frame connectors and joist hangers, are made from galvanized steel. There are many different types of connectors and they can be used for scores of different applications.

Post stirrups, or supports, and brackets (see the diagram on page 64)

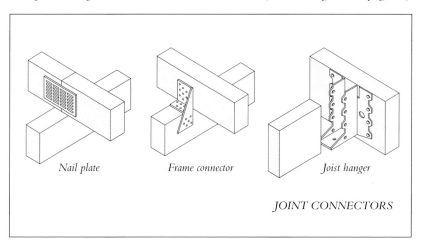

Nail plate   *Frame connector*   *Joist hanger*

JOINT CONNECTORS

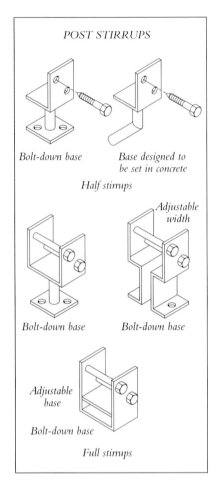

POST STIRRUPS

Bolt-down base

Base designed to be set in concrete

Half stirrups

Adjustable width

Bolt-down base

Bolt-down base

Adjustable base

Bolt-down base

Full stirrups

are hot-dipped galvanized by the manufacturer. If they are cut or drilled for any reason, reapply a protective coat of galvanized paint.

ESTIMATING MATERIALS

The plans for the deck that you have drawn up to submit to your local authority for approval, will probably have to include detailed specifications and dimensions. These drawings will help when you come to estimate the materials required for building your deck. Mistakes at this stage can be costly, as timber is expensive.

Use the materials and tools lists opposite to make a checklist of all that you will need to suit your deck. This will also help you cost the deck.

ORDERING MATERIALS

Most timber merchants will help you to order the correct quantities, grades and species of timber for your project – just show them the plan.

Timber is sold in set lengths, starting at 1.8 m and increasing in multiples of 300 mm. It may not be possible for a supplier to hold every length. Therefore, you may need to combine different measurements to avoid waste. For example, if 1.8 m joists are required and the supplier's lengths start at 2.4 m, there would be 600 mm of waste from each joist. However, the supplier may have 3.6 m lengths, in which case two joists could be obtained from each.

Decking may be purchased by the square or linear metre. Allow at least 10 per cent waste for cutting.

STORING TIMBER

When timber is delivered to the job, remember to keep it off the ground to prevent it being affected by rising moisture. Always keep it covered to protect it from rain. Moisture can cause the timber to warp or split. Keep the stack out of the way so it doesn't interfere with the smooth flow of the job.

MATERIALS CHECKLIST

Timber (specify type and size)

- Posts (or steel posts or bricks for piers)
- Ledger
- Bearers
- Joists
- Decking
- Handrailing
- Balusters
- Stair strings
- Stair treads
- Fascia boards
- Bracing
- Temporary bracing or props

Other

- Concrete for footings
- Flashing

- Drainage pipes, gravel, landscape fabric (weed mat)
- Galvanized post stirrups or brackets
- Galvanized bolts
- Capping (for brick piers)
- Galvanized bolts/coach screws with washers (for fixing bearer to post, ledger to wall, handrail to deck)
- Masonry anchors
- Lost-head galvanized nails: 100 x 3.75 mm, 75 x 3.5 mm for construction
- Twisted-shank decking nails: 50 x 3.5 mm
- Framing brackets (joist hangers)
- Nail plates
- Tie rods for stairs
- Oil finishes or stains (primers, filler, finish coats)

TOOLS

- Builders square
- Chalk line
- Chisels
- Circular saw
- Combination square
- Cramps
- Crowbar
- Electric drill and bits

- Electric plane
- Excavation machinery★
- Hammer
- Hand saw
- Nail punch
- Plumb bob
- Pneumatic nail gun and compressor★

- Post-hole shovel or auger★
- Shovel
- Spanner
- Spirit level
- String line
- Tape measure
- Water level

★ Can be hired if necessary.

Getting started

Before you begin building your deck you will need to prepare the site and set out the area for construction.

PREPARING THE SITE

If necessary, level the site, although the post heights can be adjusted to allow for uneven ground.

DRAINAGE

If you are building on clayey soil or the site is subjected to a lot of water, use a rubble drain to divert it away from the structure. The drain should be connected to an absorption pit or stormwater pipe out on to the street. It should not direct water on to a neighbouring property.

To construct a rubble drain, dig a trench around the area, allowing for a slight fall to the stormwater pipe or pit. Dig the trench 50 mm deeper than the bottom of the footing. Place 75 mm of coarse gravel or river stone in the bottom of the trench. Lay a plastic agricultural drainage pipe (slotted PVC pipe, preferably with a fine nylon screen sock over it) on top and cover it with fine gravel. Cover this with a landscape fabric (weed mat) and a layer of soil.

WEED CONTROL

Ideally, remove the top layer of soil to ensure grass and weeds don't grow through the deck. The area can also be covered with a landscape fabric and 50 mm of medium gravel. This will also help to drain the surface.

THE LEDGER

When building an attached deck, first fix the ledger to the house, tying the frame of the deck to the building and its solid foundation. The ledger must be secured at the correct height and it must be level. The height depends on whether the joists will be placed on top of it or against its face.

FIXING THE LEDGER

1 Determine the height for the top of the ledger. Allow for the thickness of the decking (usually 22 mm) and the height of the joists, if applicable. The decking should lie 25 mm below any sill, so that rainwater won't run back into the house. Use a spirit level and straight edge, or a water level and chalk line, to mark out the top of the ledger on the side of the house.

2 If the house has weatherboards, remove one or two to provide a flat surface for the ledger. Place flashing directly above the ledger to prevent water entering the house, and fit a timber spacer behind the ledger so the full width of the ledger will support the joists.

3 Use coach screws to attach the ledger to the house frame or bolt it through to the bearer or joists. Drill

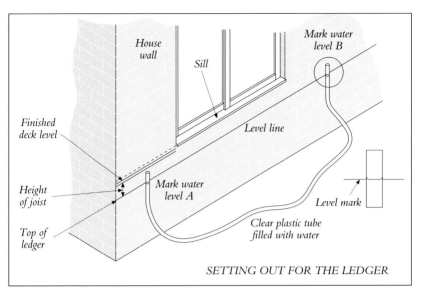

House wall

Sill

Mark water level B

Finished deck level

Level line

Height of joist

Mark water level A

Level mark

Top of ledger

Clear plastic tube filled with water

SETTING OUT FOR THE LEDGER

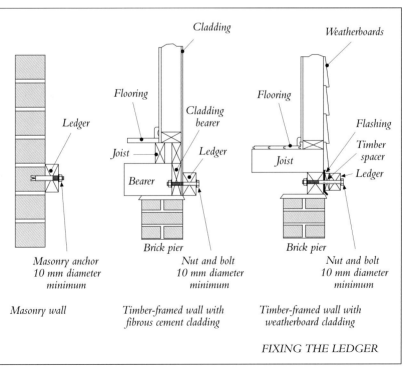

Cladding

Weatherboards

Flooring

Cladding bearer

Ledger

Joist

Ledger

Bearer

Flooring

Flashing

Timber spacer

Ledger

Joist

Brick pier

Brick pier

Masonry anchor
10 mm diameter
minimum

Nut and bolt
10 mm diameter
minimum

Nut and bolt
10 mm diameter
minimum

Masonry wall

Timber-framed wall with
fibrous cement cladding

Timber-framed wall with
weatherboard cladding

FIXING THE LEDGER

holes through the ledger for the screws, directly below where each alternate deck joist will be.

4 Hold the ledger at its correct location against the house and check that it is level. Insert a pencil through the drilled holes and mark the wall. You may need a helper or temporary props to hold the work, as accuracy is important. Insert screws or bolts.

SETTING OUT AN ATTACHED DECK

5 Tack a nail into the top of the ledger at one end. Then, tie a string line to the nail and square off the house by placing a builders square on the ground. At least one arm of the square must be level. This will give you a rough line for erecting the building profile. Measure out along this line 600 mm more than the required location of the posts.

6 Construct a building profile using pointed pegs and a horizontal cross-piece 600 mm long (see diagram opposite). The pegs must be strong enough to support the stretched

string. If the deck is too high for the profile, fix a temporary ledger (batten) to the wall while you are setting out. This should be about 300 mm above the ground, level and parallel to the ledger. Place the top of the profile in the same horizontal plane as the ledger. Remove the temporary string line.

7 Using the '3-4-5' method, square the string line off the house at the end of the ledger. Fix the string line to the profile at this position. Repeat at the other end of the ledger.

8 Erect profiles parallel to each string line and 600 mm outside them. Set up the string line for the posts by measuring the required distance from the house along the string lines. Stretch a third string line across and tie it to the outside profiles.

9 Check the string lines are parallel and at the same slope, and measure the diagonals. If they are equal, the set-out is square. Adjust as required. Attach the string line to a small nail in the top of the profile; check again.

SETTING OUT A FREE-STANDING DECK

Free-standing decks have an extra row of posts and a bearer instead of a ledger. Drive in pegs at the corners on the high side of the area. Use a string line and level to bring them to a level plane. Set out the other sides as for the attached deck, using the level line instead of the ledger.

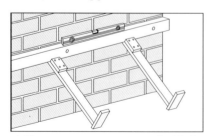

4 Use temporary props to hold the ledger at its correct location against the house and check that it is level.

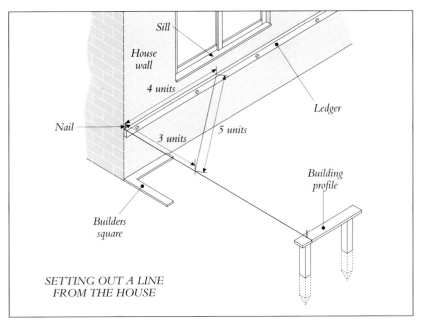

Sill

House
wall

4 units

Nail

3 units

5 units

Ledger

Builders
square

Building
profile

**SETTING OUT A LINE
FROM THE HOUSE**

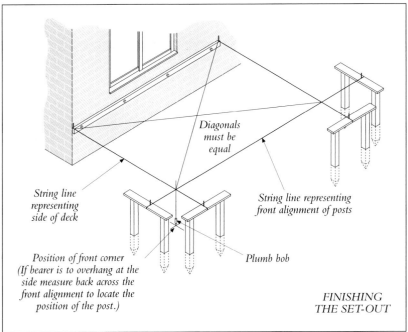

Diagonals
must be
equal

String line
representing
side of deck

String line representing
front alignment of posts

Position of front corner
(If bearer is to overhang at the
side measure back across the
front alignment to locate the
position of the post.)

Plumb bob

**FINISHING
THE SET-OUT**

The footings for this deck are concealed by attractive trellis work, which complements the arches at the top of the posts.

Footings and posts

Footings and posts provide the basic support for the deck. The posts must be strong enough to bear its weight, and the footings should be spaced correctly to make the structure solid.

FOOTINGS

A footing (normally made of concrete) is placed in the ground to stabilize the deck structure. The footing must rest on solid ground capable of carrying the load of the deck safely without any undue movement. Depending on the type of soil at your site, the size of the footing will vary (consult your local Building Control office).

If you are using timber posts, the height of the concrete footing is not important. However, the top should be approximately 50 mm above the ground and the surface graded away from the post or its support. This helps to prevent the water from welling around the post. If a timber post is to be placed in the footing, 75 mm of coarse gravel (approximately 20 mm in diameter) should be placed in the bottom of the hole.

If the deck is to rest on brick piers the footings usually finish below ground level. The precise height will depend on the pier, which must be an even number of brick courses and finish immediately below the bearer.

MAKING THE FOOTINGS

1 Set out the site (see pages 66–9). Use a permanent marker to mark the location of each post on the string line. The spacing for the posts will depend on the section, size and grade of timber used for the bearer (see table on page 61). The standard

FOOTINGS FOR BRACED DECKS★	
AREA SUPPORTED BY EACH POST★★	MINIMUM FOOTING SIZE
5 m^2	300 x 300 mm; 600 mm deep
10 m^2	600 x 600 mm; 600 mm deep
15 m^2	600 x 600 mm; 600 mm deep
20 m^2	750 x 750 mm; 600 mm deep

★ Suitable for decks up to 3.6 m above ground on minimum soil-bearing pressure of 150 kPa, such as rock, sand or gravel of medium density, or moderately stiff clay.

★ This can be calculated by multiplying the bearer span by the joist span.

spacing is 1.8 m although this may increase to 3.6 m. Using a plumb bob or spirit level, transfer these positions to the ground. This mark will represent the centre front alignment for each pier or post. Use a peg to indicate the centre of each post and remove the string line.

2 Determine the size of the footings (see the table on page 71).

3 The bottom of the footing must rest on stable ground, so remove any tree roots. Remove the top layer of dirt with a garden spade and use a post-hole shovel or auger to dig the

---

DIGGING IN SOFT SOIL

If you have sandy or soft soil that tends to fall into the hole as you dig, then cut the top and bottom from a 23 litre drum. Place the drum in position and dig through it. Push it into the excavation as you go. This drum may also be used as formwork when you are pouring the wet concrete for the footing.

To stop sandy soil falling into the hole as you dig, place a drum in position and dig through it.

---

footing holes. Hold the handles together and drive the blades into the ground a few times to break up the soil. Spread the handles to hold the soil, then lift it out and place the dirt far enough away from the excavation to avoid any falling back into the hole. (If there is a large number of holes, you can hire a powered post-hole auger; be sure to get adequate instructions from the hire company.)

4 Construct a 100 mm high timber form box and place it over the hole, centred on the post position. Fix it with pegs – you may need to brace it temporarily to hold it in the correct location. Paint the inside of the formwork with a little oil – this makes it easier to remove once the concrete has set.

5 The concrete mix should not be too wet. The consistency should be wet enough to pour, yet stiff enough to hold the post or stirrups until set. Pour the concrete mix into the form and ram it down well with a piece of timber to prevent air pockets, as they will hold water and can cause the post to rot or rust.

POSTS OR PIERS

Generally, decks are supported by posts, or by piers or columns. Timber or steel posts are the more common method of support, and they can be either round or square. Steel posts are embedded into the concrete footing while timber posts may be placed in the footing or on post stirrups (supports). Posts may extend through the top of the deck to provide support for a handrail or even a pergola (roof).

Timber posts should have a C24 stress rating if they are hardwood and at least C24 if treated softwood (see pages 56–8 and 60). For suitable timber sizes see the table on page 61. When softwood posts will be embedded in the ground, use timber with a high rating (check with your local authority about conditions in your area). Ensure you place the trimmed end up so that it is above ground level and the end in the ground is the one fully treated by the supplier. You can use brush-on preservatives but they do not have the same amount of penetration as pressure-treatment.

Piers or columns are normally made of brickwork or from reinforced concrete poured into a form tube. For high-wind areas a tie-down rod must be placed in the columns and embedded into the footing during construction.

If necessary, packing such as fibrous cement sheet can be placed on top of the pier to get the precise height for the bearer. The external face of the pier should align with the string line. On top of each pier place a damp-proof course and, particularly in areas where insects are a problem, capping. Brick piers and footings must comply with current building standards and codes.

For a narrow attached deck with ledger, only one bearer and one row

A metal stirrup supports this timber post, raising it and protecting it from rot and insect attack.

of posts are required. For a free-standing deck you need a minimum of two bearers and two rows of posts. Extra bearers and rows of posts are required for a larger deck.

ERECTING THE POSTS

1 If stirrups are to be embedded in the footing, place them in the wet concrete, ensuring they are aligned with the string line. Use a level to

HINT

Check with your local authorities for the location of underground services such as gas or water pipes, phone or electric cables. If you damage them you may not only have to pay the repair cost, but you may also be placing yourself in danger.

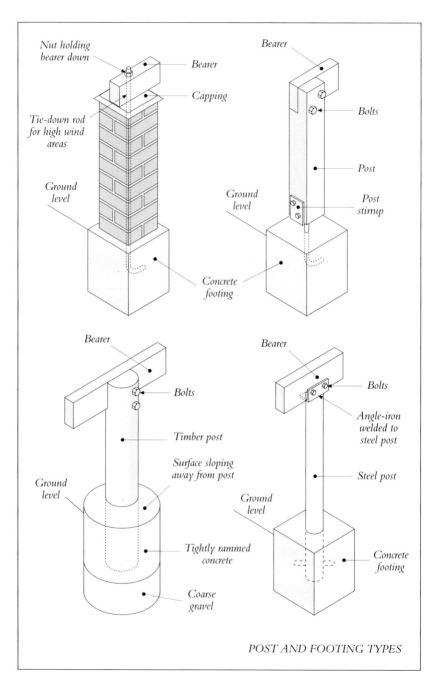

Nut holding bearer down

Bearer

Capping

Tie-down rod for high wind areas

Ground level

Concrete footing

Bearer

Bolts

Post

Post stirrup

Ground level

Concrete footing

Bearer

Bolts

Timber post

Surface sloping away from post

Ground level

Tightly rammed concrete

Coarse gravel

Bearer

Bolts

Angle-iron welded to steel post

Steel post

Ground level

Concrete footing

POST AND FOOTING TYPES

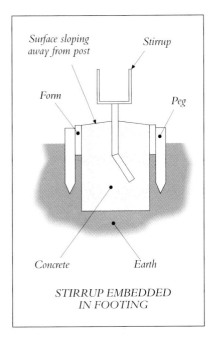

Surface sloping away from post *Stirrup*

Form *Peg*

Concrete *Earth*

STIRRUP EMBEDDED IN FOOTING

check the alignment. Alternatively, embed a treated timber or steel post in the concrete. The posts may need to be temporarily braced in position while the concrete is poured and setting. They must be perfectly vertical and in alignment, as there is no easy way to correct this once the

concrete is set. Timber posts can be cut to height after the concrete has set. Steel posts must be set in the concrete at the correct height, as they cannot be cut later. The string line should align with the position of the lower edge of the bearer or its housing. Finally, allow the concrete footings to cure for approximately seven days before continuing.

2 If you are using bolt-down stirrups, fix them in place. Take one post and stand it in a stirrup in its correct alignment with the string line. It should be a little longer than the finished post to allow for fitting and levelling. Temporarily fix the post with one nail or screw through the holes in the stirrup. This will hold the base of the post and leave the top free. Use a spirit level to check for vertical both ways and temporarily brace the post. Repeat this for the post at the opposite end and for any intermediate posts. Again, check that the posts are vertical and in alignment, and adjust them as required.

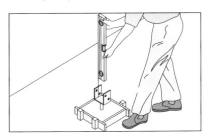

1 Place a stirrup in the wet concrete, ensuring it is aligned with the string line. Use a level to check that it is perfectly vertical and in alignment.

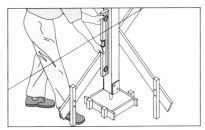

2 Stand a post in the stirrup, aligning it with the string line. Fix it temporarily with a nail or screw through the holes in the stirrup.

The ends of the joists here have been painted to match the bearer and bottom railing so that they create a decorative checked effect. A fascia board could have been used to conceal them.

The horizontal framework

A deck is a simple structure, similar to the interior floor of a house. Bearers rest on the posts and joists on the bearers, thus making the horizontal framework for the deck.

TIMBER

Bearers and joists are usually of medium durability or greater, and are of pressure-treated timber (see pages 56–8 and 60). They should have a stress rating of no less than C24. For suitable timber sizes, see the tables on pages 61–3.

BEARERS

The bearers span from post-to-post. In the case of an attached deck, the decking boards and bearers usually run parallel to the house and the ledger. For example, if you want the decking boards to run at 90 degrees from the house, you can fix the bearers to the top of the ledger at the same angle.

Bearers can be fixed to the posts in a number of ways:
• They can be housed into the posts below the level line (see pages 78–9).
• They can sit on top of the posts and be fixed with skew-nailing or, preferably, nail plates.
• Bearers can be bolted directly into the face of the post.

If desired, a pair of bearers can be attached to either side of the post with solid blocking between. In this case smaller timber sections can be used. Take care to ensure that the top edges of both bearers are at the same level and alignment, or they won't support the joists properly.

DETERMINING THE BEARER HEIGHT

Take care in determining the bearer height and levels, as you don't want a twisted, uneven or out-of-level deck. Check again that the posts are aligned and vertical, and transfer a level mark from the top of the ledger to each post. For wider decks use a water level, but on narrower decks a straight edge and spirit level may be used. Rest the spirit level in the centre of the straight edge. With one end of the straight edge resting on top of the ledger, move the other up or down until the edge is level. Mark the bottom of the straight edge on the post.
• If the joists are to be fixed on top of the ledger and bearer, this will become the top of the bearer. Transfer the mark on to the corner posts. Pull a string line tightly from each corner post and mark the bearer height on each intermediate post.
• If the joists are to be fixed at the height of the ledger but over the bearers, the bearer will need to be lower. Measure down the height of

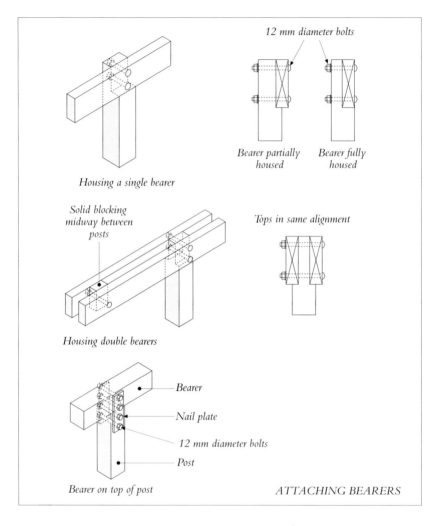

12 mm diameter bolts

Housing a single bearer

Bearer partially housed

Bearer fully housed

Solid blocking midway between posts

Tops in same alignment

Housing double bearers

Bearer

Nail plate

12 mm diameter bolts

Post

Bearer on top of post

ATTACHING BEARERS

the joists from the original mark. Make a second mark and transfer it to all the posts in the same way.

If bearers are not long enough and have to be joined end-to-end, the joint must be placed directly over a post. In the case of double bearers, the joins should be staggered. Use a scarf joint for maximum strength.

ATTACHING THE BEARERS

1 If the posts are in stirrups, number each post and stirrup to match (the post heights may vary). Place a cross on the side of the post where the bearer is to be fitted. Remove the posts from the stirrups and lay each one on a set of trestles so that you can work on them easily.

This bearer is housed into the posts, which continue up to support the railing.

2 The bearers are housed into the posts below the level line. From the line on each post measure down the height of the bearer. Square both lines across the face and down each side. Mark the depth of the housing: it is generally the thickness of the bearers or a maximum of two-thirds the thickness of the post. Cut the housings with a power saw. Clean them out with a chisel and check that they fit neatly.

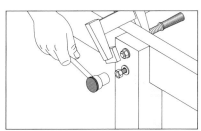

4 Drill bolt holes through the bearer into the post, apply preservative and fasten with the bolts.

3 Re-erect each post in its correct location and check that it is in alignment and vertical. Use braces to hold it in position. Fasten it to the stirrup with 10 mm bolts.

4 Place the bearer in position. Level it and secure it with a cramp. Use galvanized cuphead bolts (preferably two per post). Drill the bolt holes through the bearer into the post. The drill bit may not be long enough to go through the bearer and the post; if so, remove the bearer and continue to drill the holes all the way through. Apply a coat of preservative to both surfaces within the joint. Replace the bearer and fasten with the bolts.

JOISTS

Joists span the width of the deck and are fixed to the bearer and ledger, or two bearers, in one of several ways:

• Joists may sit on top of the bearers, and be skew-nailed or fixed with a frame connector.

• Joists may sit against the face of the bearers and ledger. Use joist hangers for maximum strength.

• Joists may fit against the face of the ledger and over the bearers.

Other types of framing brackets may also be used. If you are using joist hangers, the ledger, bearers and joist should be the same size.

The joists may finish at, or extend past, the outside bearer. Allowing them to overhang the bearer will make the deck more attractive as the posts will be set back from the edge.

The posts will also be less noticeable, especially if they are camouflaged by plants. The overhang must not exceed one-quarter of the joist span (see the diagram opposite).

Although joists are usually laid at right angles to bearers this can vary, for example if you are laying decking boards in a pattern (see page 86).

ATTACHING JOISTS

1 Mark the spacings for each joist on top of the ledger and bearers by measuring along both from the same end. This will ensure that the joists are parallel, whether or not the spacings between them are even. The

FIXING TO A ROUND POST

1 To house a bearer into a round post, first measure the thickness of the bearer back from the front edge. Then mark this thickness across the top of each post, measuring from the front. Pull a string line across the top of the row of posts to represent the back of the housing.

2 Draw a vertical line down each side of the post the height of the bearer. Use a square piece of cardboard as a guide and mark a line around the post.

3 Cut the housing with a hand saw for safety and remove the waste with a chisel.

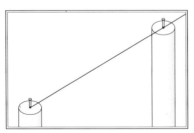

1 Measure the thickness of the bearer back from the front edge and pull a string line across the posts.

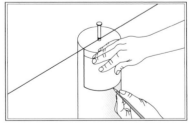

2 Use a square piece of cardboard to mark the line for the bottom of the housing around the post.

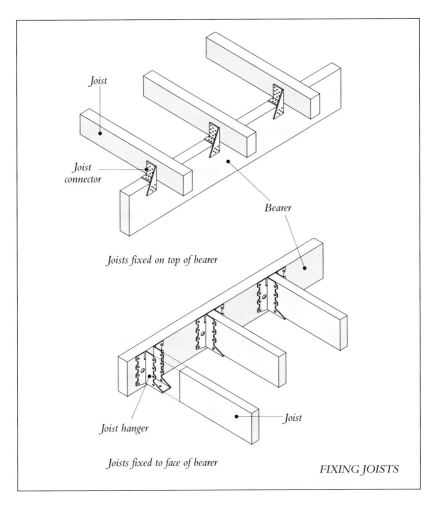

Joist

Joist connector

Bearer

Joists fixed on top of bearer

Joist hanger

Joist

Joists fixed to face of bearer

FIXING JOISTS

maximum recommended spacing will not always suit your deck. You can either adjust it and keep all the spacing the same, or adjust the two end spaces only. Never exceed the maximum recommended spacing (see the tables on pages 62–3).

2 Square the spacings down the face of the ledger and place a cross to mark the position of the joist. Using galvanized 30 x 2.8 mm clout nails or those recommended by the manufacturer, fix one side of the hanger to the ledger or bearer. Position it so that the joist and ledger are flush on top. Use an offcut of joist material to help position the hanger (this will be easier than manoeuvring a joist).

3 Square the ledger end of the two
outside joists. Do not cut them to
finished length unless they are to fit
between the ledger and the bearer. If
they sit over the bearer they are
trimmed later. Apply a preservative
and fit the joist in the hanger. Fix the
other side of the hanger to the ledger
and then fix it to the joist. If the
joists sit on top of the ledger, leave a
10 mm gap between the end of the
joist and the wall.

4 Check that the posts are still
vertical and aligned. Skew-nail the
other end of the joist to the top of
the bearer with one 75 x 3.5 mm
galvanized nail, or temporarily fix a
hanger in place.

5 Measure the diagonals of the
structure for square and adjust as
required. You may need to use a
temporary brace to hold the structure
square. When you are satisfied, finish
fixing the end joists and all those
remaining, keeping any bows in the
timber at the top.

6 If the joists overhang, mark the
required length on each end joist and
stretch a string line between them.
Draw vertical lines down the sides of
each one to correspond with the
string line, and cut them to length.

FINISHING THE
FRAMEWORK

7 If desired, fix a fascia board over
the ends of the joists to give the deck
a neater finish. The board must be
well secured if a handrail is to be
attached to it.

8 Fix any necessary bracing (see the
box opposite). Once these braces are
permanently fixed, any temporary
bracing that was used to hold the
structure square during construction
may be removed.

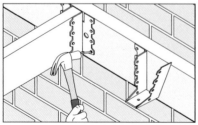

*3 Fix one side of the hanger to the
ledger, square the end of the joist,
then fix the other side of the hanger.*

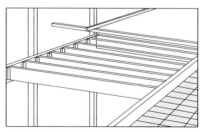

*5 Fix temporary braces to hold the
structure square and finish fixing the
joists in position.*

BRACING THE DECK

A deck that is securely fixed to a house, especially in a corner, will require only minimal bracing, if any. A deck higher than 1200 mm should have at least a pair of opposing braces. Decks higher than 1800 mm and wider than 2000 mm need a pair of opposing braces in both directions. Any deck built in a high-wind area or that is free-standing on stirrups should also be braced.

A simple 100 x 50 mm timber brace at 45 degrees (from post to bearer and secured with bolts) will be adequate in most situations. The brace angle may vary up to 5 degrees, but the bottom of the brace should not be lower than half the post height.

For taller or free-standing decks, cross-bracing from the top of one post to the bottom of the next will provide better stability.

The bracing will not necessarily detract from the appearance of the deck, as it can be concealed with lattice, vertical or horizontal battens or a trellis for a climbing vine. Fix the diagonal bracing under the joists with halving joints in the centre. Use 90 x 45 mm timbers and bolt them at each end with a 12 mm diameter bolt. Nail them to each joist.

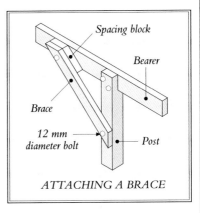

ATTACHING A BRACE

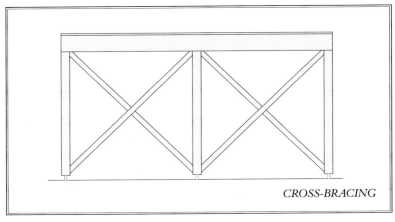

CROSS-BRACING

The decking

The decking is the part of a deck most often seen, and so selection of the timber and accurate fixing is a crucial part of building such a structure.

DECKING BOARDS

The decking boards are fixed on top of the joists parallel to the bearers. They must be spaced a little apart to allow water to pass through.

Decking boards come in various sizes, the two most common being machined from 100 x 25 mm or 75 x 25 mm timber. They are suitable for 450 mm joist spacings. Other sizes may be machined to order.

Decking is subjected to weather and traffic and so must be good quality timber. Use either seasoned hardwood with medium durability or treated softwood with a medium rating or greater. Decking should be free of structural defects, especially splits and knots. Cup-faced boards should be laid with the cup down to prevent anyone tripping on them.

Most timber suppliers will have a selection of decking boards, varying in durability, grading, shapes and, of course, price. Decking is usually purchased by the square or lineal metre; allow 10 per cent for wastage.

Don't use short lengths: the boards must span at least three joists. Fluted or skid-resistant boards are best as they are attractive and make the gaps between boards less obvious. They should be used around pools.

The most commonly used decking profiles have rounded top edges that are splinter-free, more even to walk on and accept stain more readily.

HINT
Add a coat of preservative or stain before the boards are nailed down. It's also a good idea to apply a coat to the tops of joists and other hard-to-reach spots.

DECKING SPANS★		
	THICKNESS	MAXIMUM JOIST SPACING
Hardwood	19 mm	500 mm
	25 mm	650 mm
Treated softwood	22 mm	450 mm

★ Standard-grade timbers. The spans for different designs are given in the diagram on page 86.

Decking boards should be securely fixed and properly spaced to provide a safe and comfortable floor for a deck.

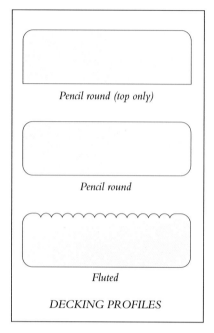

Pencil round (top only)

Pencil round

Fluted

DECKING PROFILES

DECKING PATTERNS

Decking is usually laid parallel to the house, but laying it at different angles can give a more interesting effect. This takes longer and costs more, but the result will be well worth it.

If you are laying a pattern, the placement and direction of the joists will need to be worked out to accommodate it. To ensure a solid surface where decking is joined, use double joists. The joist spacing should be calculated in the direction in which the decking is to be laid, not square off the joists.

LAYING THE DECKING

1 Cut the tops of all the joists flush and remove any bows that project too high. Check the frame with a

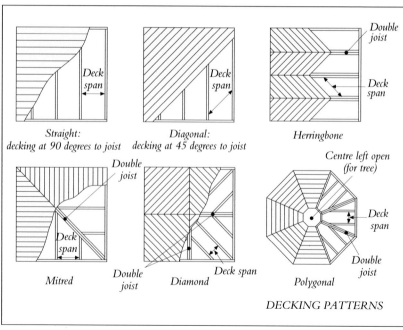

Straight:
decking at 90 degrees to joist

Diagonal:
decking at 45 degrees to joist

Herringbone

Mitred

Diamond

Polygonal

DECKING PATTERNS

long straight edge and trim the tops of the joists with a power plane.

2 Select the straightest decking board to start with, as this will determine the position of all the others. Allow the board to extend past the finished length (it will be trimmed later). The deck will look better if it has a 10–25 mm overhang on all outside edges (see the diagram on page 88). To determine the placement of the first board, subtract the overhang from the width of the board. Therefore, a board of 66 mm width with an overhang on the outside edge of 10 mm will have a starter width of 56 mm. Measure in 56 mm from the outside edge at both ends and stretch and snap a chalk line between these two points. This will provide a straight line to start on.

3 Secure the first board in line with the chalk mark. Using twisted-shank nails (see page 62), nail from one end to the other, straightening the board as you go. Drive in two nails per joist at a slight angle and punch the heads below the surface.

● If there are handrail posts you may have to secure the first board further in from the edge to clear the posts. In this case, the starting position should match equal board widths and gaps from the outside. The decking can be cut in around the posts later.

● At the ends of the boards drill pilot holes to prevent them from splitting. Drill the pilot hole slightly smaller than the nail diameter. You may also need to drill holes through the decking if the timber is too dry and likely to split.

● To save time, you can use a powered nail gun. Ensure the nails are suitable for use in the gun.

4 Scatter a number of boards on the joist at a time to provide a work platform. Position the next board against the first board with its end extending past the finished length. It will be trimmed off later. Leave a small gap (3–4 mm) between the boards for drainage and to allow dirt to fall through. (This gap may seem small, but the timber will shrink over time.) A nail can be used as a spacer to maintain the gap. Use a spacer at

1 Check the frame with a long straight edge and trim the tops of the joists with a power plane.

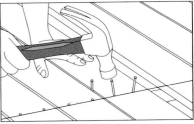

4 Use a nail as a spacer and drive in two nails per joist at a slight angle. Punch the heads below the surface.

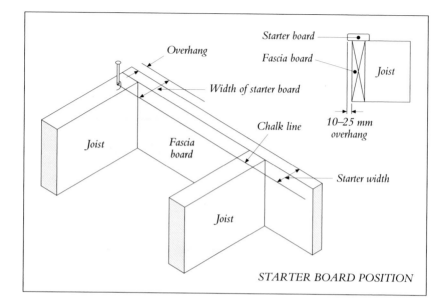

Overhang

Starter board

Fascia board

Joist

Width of starter board

10–25 mm overhang

Chalk line

Joist

Fascia board

Joist

Starter width

Joist

STARTER BOARD POSITION

one end and another in close proximity to the joist that the decking is being nailed to. Nail the boards down as for the first board.

5 Straighten bowed decking boards as you work.

• If the board bows in, nail one end in place. Work along the board, placing the spacer to create the required gap. At the bow, drive a chisel into the top of the joist and lever the board over to the spacer. Nail down. Continue this from joist-to-joist. Look along the board to check for straightness.

• If the board is bowed out, secure each end with the correct spacing. Then, place a spacer in the centre of the bow. Use the chisel to lever the board over and nail. Repeat this on both sides of each joist. Check the

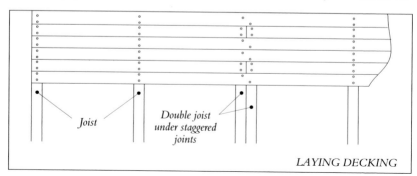

Joist

Double joist under staggered joints

LAYING DECKING

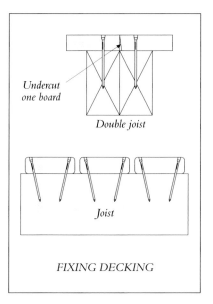

Undercut one board

Double joist

Joist

FIXING DECKING

the remaining gaps slightly to make any adjustment.

7 Stagger joins, and if possible support them on double joists. To obtain a tight fit, one of the ends can be undercut slightly.

TRIMMING DECKING ENDS

8 Mark the overhang at each end of the deck, that is on the first and last boards. Measure the distance from the blade of your circular saw to the outside edge of the base plate. Mark this distance in from the overhang position and secure a straight edge as a guide for the saw to run against. Look along the guide and straighten it if required by nailing at regular intervals. Alternatively, snap a chalk line between the two overhang points and cut along this line. However, this method does require greater accuracy in use of the saw.

9 Place the circular saw against the straight edge and trim the overhang. Round over the trimmed ends with a hand plane or router. Sand the boards if required.

board for straightness and continue the process as required.

6 Regularly check the decking for parallel, especially the remaining spacing. Measure at each end and in the centre. If the spacing is not parallel, adjust the gaps over the next few boards, and re-check the measurements. To avoid finishing with uneven boards or spacing, check your measurements on the last 900 mm or so. Then, open or close

HINT
When using a nail as a spacer, drive it through a piece of thin timber to prevent it repeatedly falling between the boards. Use three spacers – one at each end and one where you are working.

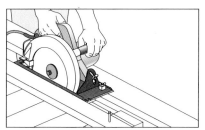

8 Trim the ends of the decking boards using a circular saw with a straight edge nailed to the deck as a guide.

Stairs are essential for providing easy access to the garden from any deck apart from those right on ground level.

Deck stairs

Whether the deck is attached or free-standing, it will in most cases need stairs for access to the garden and perhaps between levels. A basic open stair is all that is needed.

DESIGNING DECK STAIRS

Stairs for a deck should not be elaborate, as fine detailing can trap moisture and cause rot. Use a concrete pad or footings under the strings to keep them above the ground and away from moisture.

A comfortable width for a stair is about 900 mm and it should not be less than 760 mm. If it is wider than 900 mm it will require a string (centre carriage piece) for support.

The string tops can be fixed by one of two methods (see page 94):

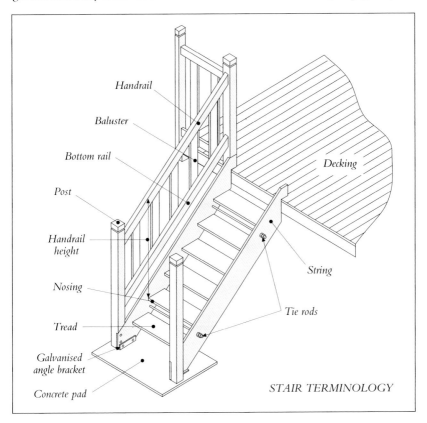

Handrail

Baluster

Bottom rail

Post

Handrail height

Nosing

Tread

Galvanised angle bracket

Concrete pad

Decking

String

Tie rods

STAIR TERMINOLOGY

• cutting hooks in the end of the string to sit on the joist or decking;

• cutting the end to fit against the face of the joist and holding it in place with a ledger or angle brackets.

PARTS OF THE STAIRS

• Strings. These are the main support for the stairs. There is one on each side spanning from the deck to the ground. The treads are attached to them. Strings may have a sawtooth shape or a straight top. The timber used should be as straight as possible and free from any defects.

• Treads. These are the steps. To create a horizontal surface to walk on, they are attached to strings on both sides, either the top of sawtoothed strings or the face of the strings. They can be housed into the string or secured to them on timber supports or steel brackets (see page 95). Two pieces of timber laid side-by-side to obtain the required tread width are better than one wide piece, as wider pieces are more prone to distortion when exposed to the weather. The nosing is the front of the tread and the going is the clear tread width.

• Riser. This is the vertical distance between the top of one tread and the the next (the height of each step). Internal stairs may have a riser board placed between the treads but this is not common on external stairs. The total 'rise' is the effective height of all the risers added together.

Your local Building Control office will have regulations for building stairs and these will ensure that you construct a comfortable and safe stairway. Some of the regulations in the Building Regulations (1991) (Part K) include:

• All the rise measurements in the stairway must be the same and measure between 220 and 115 mm.

• Treads must have a clear width of between 220 and 355 mm.

• The relation between tread and risers must be such that:

2R + G = between 550 and 700 mm (where R = riser and G = going or clear tread width)

The regulations also state that a stair over 600 mm in height or more than five risers must have a handrail not less than 900 mm high.

MEASURING UP

1 To determine the rise and going of your stairs, measure the distance from the top of the decking to the ground. Be sure the measurement is taken vertical from the top and not at an angle. For example, the distance might be 1200 mm.

2 Divide this measurement by 175 mm (average riser height), then round it to the nearest whole number, for example 1200 divided by 175 = 6.86 or 7 risers. Now divide 1200 by 7 to find the finished riser height (171 mm).

3 To check that this riser height is acceptable, decide on a going (275 mm is average) and use the 2R + G formula: (2 x 171) + 275 = 617 mm, which fits the formula.

4 There is one less tread than risers (the top of the deck is not considered a tread). Therefore, in our example there would be 6 treads. The total going would be 6 x 275 = 1650 mm.

5 The length of the string forms the hypotenuse of a right-angled triangle where the other two sides are the total going and the total rise (see the diagram below). The formula is $a^2 + b^2 = c^2$, where a is the total going, b is the total rise and c is the length of the string. Therefore, in the following example, $1650^2 + 1200^2 =$ the length squared (2040.221^2). The length of the string is then rounded off to 2040 mm.

CONSTRUCTING THE LANDING PAD

6 Set out the pad. The position is determined by measuring out horizontally from the face of the deck, the total going of the stair (for example, 1650 mm). The pad will need to be a little closer to the deck (about 300 mm) so the strings rest on it. It should be a little wider than, and extend in front of, both strings (so that you can step on it), and be about 100 mm deep.

7 Excavate and place a form in the area for the pad. Pour the concrete and leave it to set for at least 48 hours. Galvanized angle brackets to

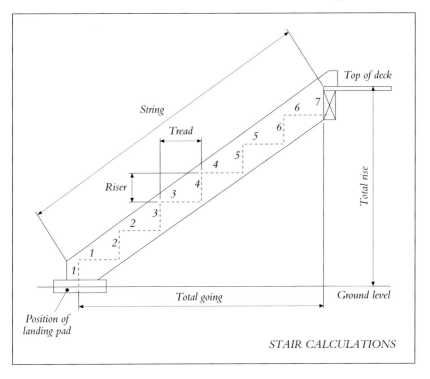

STAIR CALCULATIONS

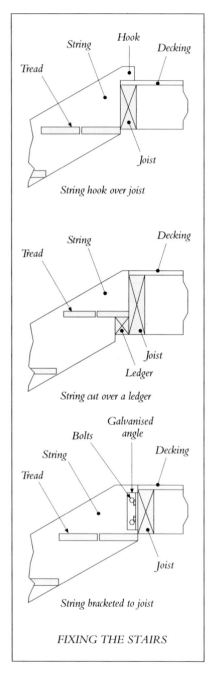

String hook over joist

String cut over a ledger

String bracketed to joist

FIXING THE STAIRS

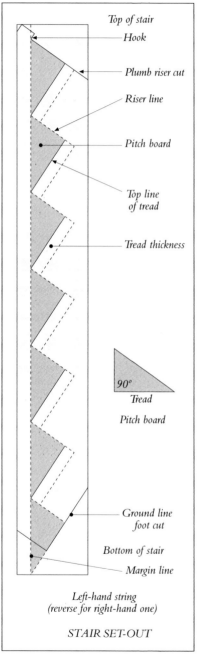

*Left-hand string
(reverse for right-hand one)*

STAIR SET-OUT

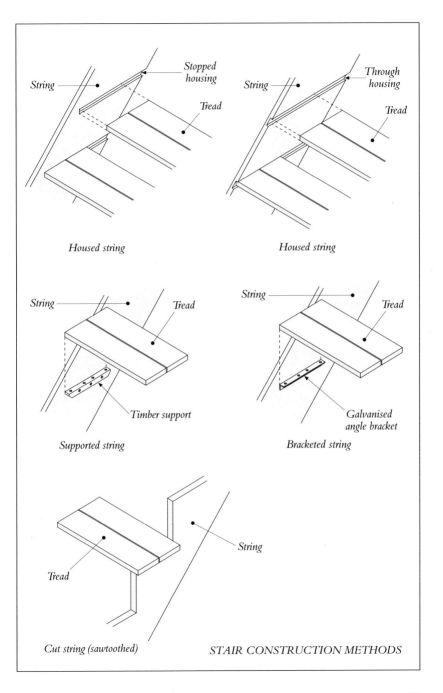

Housed string

Stopped housing

String

Tread

Housed string

Through housing

String

Tread

Supported string

String

Tread

Timber support

Bracketed string

String

Tread

Galvanised angle bracket

Cut string (sawtoothed)

Tread

String

STAIR CONSTRUCTION METHODS

hold the strings may be cast in the pad, or bolted on later.

8 Use a straight edge and level to determine the new rise height from the top of the pad. Divide the height by the number of risers (7) to find the finished height of each.

MARKING OUT THE STAIRS

9 Decide on the type of stair you want and cut a 'pitch board' template from plywood or thick cardboard, to represent one riser and one tread.

10 Cut two strings from 300 x 50 mm timber, cutting them longer than the calculation to allow for vertical cuts and hooks at the top and a level foot at the bottom (see page 94). Place the two strings side-by-side. Mark a margin line on the face parallel to the top edge (not required if a sawtooth shape is being used).

11 Start about 50 mm in from one end of the string and trace around the template, moving it along the margin line for each tread and riser. Turn the template over and repeat on the other string. At the top, mark a hook if required. Mark the thickness of the treads.

12 Cut the housings in the strings to receive the treads with a power saw or router and carefully clean out with a chisel. Alternatively, fix brackets or supports to the face of the strings, or cut the top of each string in a saw-tooth shape.

13 Cut the end of the string as required, ensuring you have a pair (one left-hand and one right-hand).

14 Cut the treads to length. Check the fit in each housing and adjust as required. Slightly round or bevel each long edge with a hand plane. Apply a water repellent or stain to housings and end grains.

15 Stairs with more than four treads may be very heavy to manoeuvre, so fix only the top and bottom treads with 75 x 3.75 mm galvanized lost-head nails or screws. The remaining treads will be fixed later.

16 Position the stairs and secure the strings to the joist at the top and the angle bracket at the bottom. The rest of the treads may now be fixed.

17 If the stair is not directly against a wall, place a number of threaded tie rods across the stair directly under the treads at 1350 mm centres maximum. Use washers and nuts on both sides of each string to hold the rods in place.

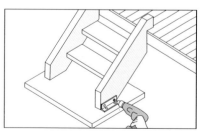

16 Position the stairs and secure the strings to the joist at the top and the angle bracket at the bottom.

DECK FURNITURE

Outdoor furniture can help you make the most of your deck. There is a large variety of ready-made timber furniture available, and you can choose timbers that match your decking material. Alternatively, you can purchase timber without a finish so you can apply one that matches your deck.

Benches can also be built as part of the deck structure. They can be fixed directly to the joist below the decking or attached to the posts around the edge of the deck (as in the diagram below). However, seating attached to the edge of the deck is not a substitute for a handrail and balustrades. The handrail should be higher behind a bench so that anyone (especially children) standing on it does not fall over the edge.

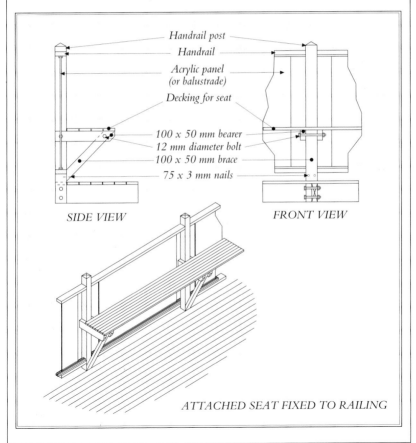

Handrail post

Handrail

Acrylic panel (or balustrade)

Decking for seat

100 x 50 mm bearer
12 mm diameter bolt
100 x 50 mm brace
75 x 3 mm nails

SIDE VIEW   *FRONT VIEW*

ATTACHED SEAT FIXED TO RAILING

Handrails

Handrailing can transform a plain-looking deck into an architectural masterpiece. However, it should blend in with its surroundings, as it will be the first part of the deck that people notice.

HANDRAIL REGULATIONS

In the interests of safety, any handrail must be securely fixed and built to current regulations. Check with your local authority, which will have regulations similar to these:

• Stairs over 600 mm or five risers high must have a handrail 900 mm or more above the front edge of the tread.

• Floors (decking) more than 600 mm above ground or floor level must have a handrail at least 900 mm high.

• Floors more than 3 m above ground or floor level must have a handrail at least 1 m high.

• The maximum recommended span for handrails varies according to the size of the timber used and whether there is a balustrade (see the tables at right and on page 100).

• The maximum space between balusters must not exceed 100 mm.

• Handrails are required on both sides of stairs and ramps when these are over 1 m wide.

THE STRUCTURE

There are many handrail designs, but all must have firmly secured posts and top rails. A bottom rail and balusters usually give extra support.

In some deck designs the posts extend from the footing through the

MAXIMUM HANDRAIL SPANS (NO BALUSTRADE)

	Max. span (mm)		
Timber (mm)	C16	C24	Oak
170 x 25			1000
190 x 25		900	1000
70 x 35		900	1000
90 x 35	900	1000	1200
120 x 35	1100	1200	1400
140 x 35	1200	1300	1500
170 x 35	1300	1400	1600
190 x 35	1400	1500	1700
220 x 35	1500	1600	1900
240 x 35	1600	1700	2000
70 x 45	1200	1300	1500
90 x 45	1400	1500	1700
120 x 45	1600	1700	2000
140 x 45	1800	1900	2200
170 x 45	1900	2100	2300
190 x 45	2100	2200	2400
220 x 45	2200	2300	2500
240 x 45	2200	2300	2500
65 x 65	2100	2200	2400
70 x 70	2300	2400	2600
90 x 70	2500	2600	2800

For any deck more than 600 mm above the ground, a securely fixed handrail is essential in order to prevent accidents. Here, lattice infill is used to give an attractive finish with an outdoor feel.

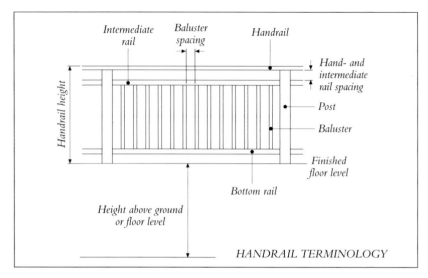

Intermediate rail
Baluster spacing
Handrail
Handrail height
Hand- and intermediate rail spacing
Post
Baluster
Finished floor level
Bottom rail
Height above ground or floor level

HANDRAIL TERMINOLOGY

MAXIMUM HANDRAIL SPANS (WITH BALUSTRADE★)

TIMBER (mm)	MAX. SPAN (mm)		
	C16	C24	OAK
70 x 35	1700	1800	2100
90 x 35	2300	2400	2600
120 x 35	2900	3000	3300
140 x 35	3200	3400	3700
170 x 35	3400	3600	4000
190 x 35	3600	3800	
70 x 45	1900	2100	2300
90 x 45	2500	2600	2800
120 x 45	3100	3200	3500
140 x 45	3500	3600	3900
170 x 45	4000		
190 x 45	4000		

★ Provide vertical support at 900 mm centres maximum.

decking to support the handrail. This is by far the strongest method. Otherwise, handrail posts must be fixed to the joists. (The tables on page 98 and at left give the maximum permissable handrail spans and, therefore, the spacings for the posts.) Note that, for reasons of space, in these two tables 'oak' is a shorthand for 'hardwood'.

Timber for handrail posts should not be smaller than 70 x 70 mm or 90 x 45 mm, with a stress rating of C24. House the bottom of the post over the joist and secure it at the base with two 10 mm diameter bolts. Use a level to keep them vertical.

Handrails and bottom rails may be fixed to the face of the posts or housed into the sides and secured with galvanized nails or screws.

Balustrades are fitted between the handrail and deck or bottom rail to form a safety screen and decoration.

The handrail should blend in with its surroundings and meet the requirements of the building regulations. Some common designs are shown on page 103.

CONSTRUCTING A HANDRAIL

The handrail and balustrade are installed after the decking and stairs have been fixed.

1 Mark a level line on one end post to represent the top edge of the handrail. Transfer it to the other end post with a water level. Snap a chalk line between to transfer the height on to any intermediate posts. Trim the posts to height (this may be above or below the line depending on your design). Locate the position for the bottom rail (if required) by measuring down from the top set-out line. Square these lines across the sides of the posts and mark a 10 mm deep housing at each location to receive the rails. With some designs the rails are simply screwed or bolted to the face of the posts, and corners are either mitred or overlapped.

2 Apply a coat of preservative (stain or paint) and nail or screw the rails into their housing (see the diagram on page 102). Shaped handrails are best secured to the posts with pipe dowels and two screws from underneath to prevent the rails twisting. To prevent the bottom rail bowing down over a large span, a blocking piece is placed between it and the deck.

3 Space the balusters evenly along the railing with 100 mm maximum between them. To calculate the spacings, add the width of one baluster (say, 40 mm) to 100 mm:

40 + 100 = 140 mm

Divide the distance between the posts (say, 2000 mm) by this and round the result up to a whole number:

2000 ÷ by 140 = 14.28, rounded up to 15 balusters

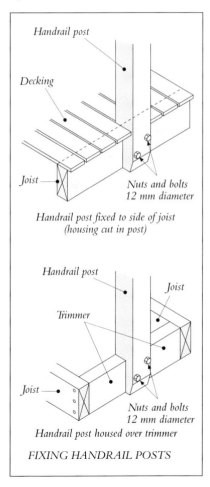

Handrail post

Decking

Joist

Nuts and bolts 12 mm diameter

Handrail post fixed to side of joist (housing cut in post)

Handrail post

Joist

Trimmer

Joist

Nuts and bolts 12 mm diameter

Handrail post housed over trimmer

FIXING HANDRAIL POSTS

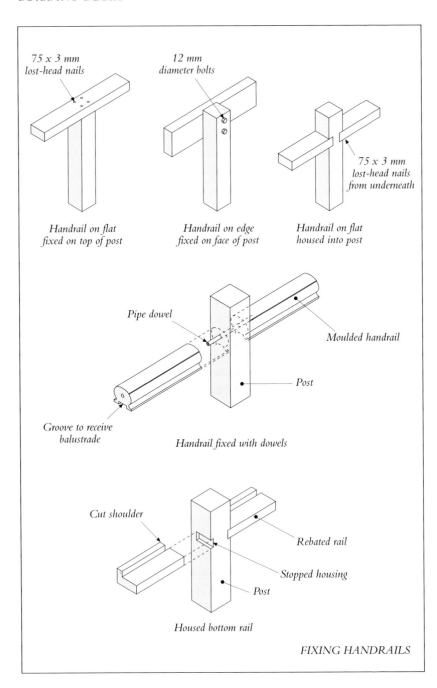

75 x 3 mm
lost-head nails

12 mm
diameter bolts

75 x 3 mm
lost-head nails
from underneath

Handrail on flat
fixed on top of post

Handrail on edge
fixed on face of post

Handrail on flat
housed into post

Pipe dowel

Moulded handrail

Post

Groove to receive
balustrade

Handrail fixed with dowels

Cut shoulder

Rebated rail

Stopped housing

Post

Housed bottom rail

FIXING HANDRAILS

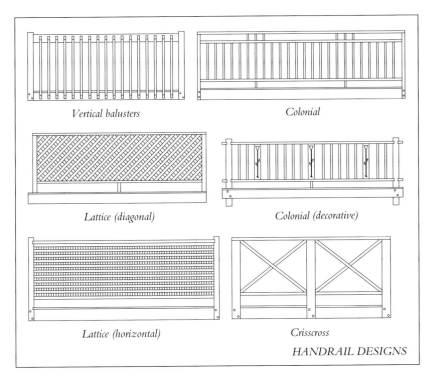

Vertical balusters

Colonial

Lattice (diagonal)

Colonial (decorative)

Lattice (horizontal)

Crisscross

HANDRAIL DESIGNS

Multiply the result by the width of one baluster:

15 x 40 = 600 mm

Subtract the result from the distance between the posts:

2000 − 600 = 1400 mm

Divide by the number of spacings required (15, one more than the number of balusters):

1400 ÷ 15 = 96 mm, which is the spacing required

4 Cut a piece of timber to this width to act as a spacer. Place the first baluster in position with the spacer between the baluster and the handrail post, ensuring it fits neatly into any grooves or rebates on the rails.

Before fixing, check for vertical. Secure at the top and base with nails or screws. Continue to move the spacer and fix each baluster in turn. Once you are about halfway, check the gap to ensure your spacings are correct. Adjust as required.

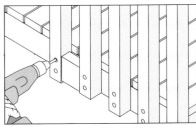

4 Move the spacer and fix each baluster in turn, securing it at the top and bottom with nails or screws.

A finished deck will need a good, protective finish in order to withstand the elements of nature. Especially formulated decking stains or oils can be used for either a natural look or to change the colour of the timber.

Finishing the deck

Decks are exposed to the weather and so need to be given a protective finish. This will ensure that the timber lasts longer and the structure remains in good condition.

PROTECTING TIMBER

The surface of all exterior timber will eventually become weathered and discoloured, and even split or crack. Rot and mildew are more serious effects of weathering. To help counteract it, apply a water repellent and a finish coat of oil or paint.

• Most water repellents provide limited protection and need to be applied every six months or so. The repellent penetrates the surface of the timber without altering its natural colour, although pigments may be added. Other additives, such as ultraviolet stabilisers, insecticide and fungicides, can be incorporated for greater protection.

• Especially formulated decking stains or oils can be used for a natural look or to change the colour of the timber. Both stains and oils provide protection for up to three years, or even longer depending on the conditions. They are easy to apply and maintain and don't peel, crack or blister like some paints do. Stains will perform better when the surface has had a primer coat of water repellent.

• Any paint used should be specially formulated for external timberwork: ordinary house paint will not withstand the constant exposure to the weather. Paint manufacturers make special paint for decking.

METHOD

1 Make sure the timber is dry or the finish may blister or crack. To test, splash a handful of water across the boards. If the water is absorbed by the timber within a few minutes, the timber is dry. However, if the water remains on the surface for some time, the timber is wet and needs time to dry out before finishing. This could take up to a week or more.

2 If the timber has discoloured patches, remove them by sanding or washing the timber down with a timber bleach. To eliminate minor defects such as marks, splintering or rough surfaces, lightly sand the surface and then ensure it is free of dust or oil before finishing. Pressure-treated timber may have powdery deposits on the surface. Remove them by lightly washing the surface with mild soap and water.

3 Using a paint brush or roller, apply the finish. Keep an even amount on the surface and work the edges so that they remain wet, to avoid a streaky or patchy appearance.

The blue and white colour scheme used on the balustrade here cleverly reflects the poolside ambience.

Pool decks

Decks can make ideal surrounds for swimming pools, as they ensure a non-slip surface that is comfortable and not too hot to walk on, even on the hottest day.

BUILDING A POOL DECK
If you have an above-ground pool or one that has been constructed on a sloping site, a timber deck is an ideal way of providing access to the water.

A pool deck is constructed in the same way as any deck, but there are a few extra points to consider:
• Prepare the ground below the deck so water will drain away. One way is to lay landscape fabric on the ground and cover it with river pebbles.

• When laying the decking boards, leave a small gap between them to allow water to drain away and prevent 'ponding' on the surface.
• As the deck will be subjected to constant splashes while the pool is in use, as well as rain, it should be constructed of timber that has been treated with a water repellent.
• For decks around salt-water pools all fittings should be of stainless steel or hot-dipped galvanised metal.

Tools for building decks

Some of the most useful tools for building decks are shown below. Build up your tool kit gradually – most of the tools can be purchased from your local hardware store.

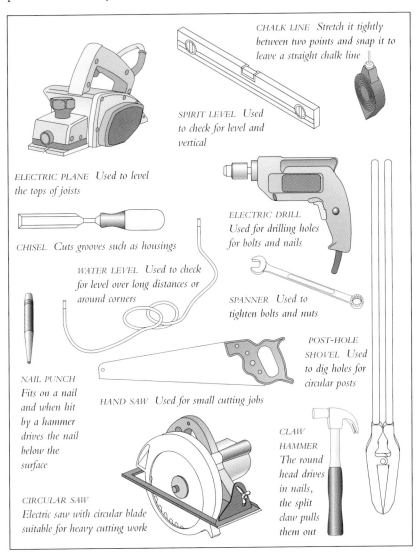

CHALK LINE *Stretch it tightly between two points and snap it to leave a straight chalk line*

SPIRIT LEVEL *Used to check for level and vertical*

ELECTRIC PLANE *Used to level the tops of joists*

CHISEL *Cuts grooves such as housings*

ELECTRIC DRILL *Used for drilling holes for bolts and nails*

WATER LEVEL *Used to check for level over long distances or around corners*

SPANNER *Used to tighten bolts and nuts*

POST-HOLE SHOVEL *Used to dig holes for circular posts*

NAIL PUNCH *Fits on a nail and when hit by a hammer drives the nail below the surface*

HAND SAW *Used for small cutting jobs*

CLAW HAMMER *The round head drives in nails, the split claw pulls them out*

CIRCULAR SAW *Electric saw with circular blade suitable for heavy cutting work*

Building
pergolas

Planning your pergola

A pergola creates fresh opportunities for enjoying outdoor space, encouraging you to utilize your garden and appreciate its views. Pergolas are usually designed to blend with existing buildings and enlarge the living area of the home.

WHAT IS A PERGOLA?

In general terms, a pergola is any horizontal trellis or framework supported on posts to form a covered walkway. The noun 'pergola' owes its origin to the Latin words *pergula* (meaning a projection or roof) and the verb *pergere* (to go forward).

Polycarbonate or metal sheeting, wooden shingles or battens, awning cloth, ceramic roof tiles or even leafy climbing plants can be added to provide various degrees of overhead protection from sun and rain for people using the structure. Full or half walls of timber lattice, wooden railings or foliage (either evergreen or deciduous) can be installed to increase privacy and screen out unwanted sun and wind, and many pergolas are erected above a wooden deck or an area of paving.

HINT

When timber is delivered to your site, stack it well clear of the surrounding soil (preferably on strips of scrap wood) to prevent moisture rising from the ground. Always cover the pile with a tarpaulin to keep it dry in wet weather, as moisture absorption can cause warping and splitting. Choose the intended position of your stack carefully to avoid interfering with the smooth flow of traffic around the site once work begins, and ensure it does not encroach on a driveway or other access route required for the delivery of ready-mix concrete or other heavy materials.

STARTING OUT

For many pergola builders, timber is the material of choice: it is readily available, relatively inexpensive and easy to use.

When planning a project, there are a few factors to consider.

• Take full advantage of the sunlight by positioning your pergola as close as possible to the ideal location on the southern side of the house.

• Note the angle of the shadows cast by existing structures or trees as the sun moves through the sky at various times of the year and see how this will affect the pergola.

• Compensate for the site's exposure to prevailing winds or poor weather. A covered pergola can provide shelter from wind and rain if a sturdy

Position your pergola to extend a living area or create a new setting for alfresco dining or relaxation. This combined pergola and deck opens off the kitchen to provide easy access for catering purposes, and doubles as a walkway to the garden.

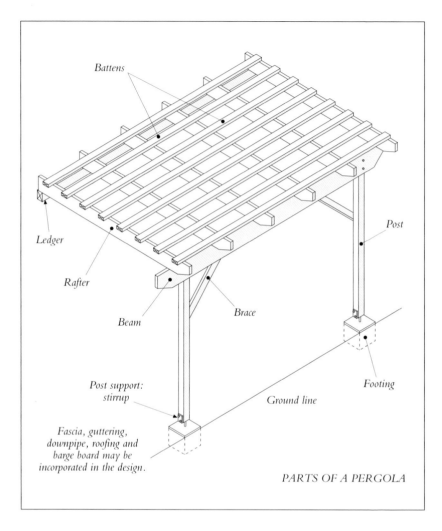

Battens

Ledger

Rafter

Beam

Post

Brace

Post support:
stirrup

Footing

Ground line

Fascia, guttering,
downpipe, roofing and
barge board may be
incorporated in the design.

PARTS OF A PERGOLA

screen is erected on the 'bad weather' side.

• Add louvred or lattice screens to restrict unsightly views and enhance privacy without compromising the through-flow of air.

• Determine the finished size of your pergola according to the area available and its intended use, working within your financial budget. Plan your project to meet individual needs. Do you require an all-weather play area for children, an entertainment venue for small or large groups, an outdoor cooking or barbecue setting, or simply a spot for quiet relaxation, either alone or with a few friends?

• The outward appearance of your proposed structure is equally important. Will it blend with its surroundings and complement existing buildings? Is it accessible to users?

Once you have identified its intended use and determined the desired size of your project, mock up a full-sized plan using lengths of timber laid out flat on the ground. Alternatively, use a pliable length of rope or even a long garden hose to represent the pergola's outline.

Test the practicality of the layout by positioning tables, chairs, lounges, barbecues and other items of furniture within the makeshift border. With these in place, is it possible for users to move around in comfort? Is there sufficient room in which to enjoy your pergola? If the answer is 'no', consider increasing its size or changing the shape. Make yourself aware of the full range of options in the early days of the design phase, well before construction begins.

Pergolas come in many shapes and sizes and are often purpose-built to suit unusual space constraints. With its segmented and slatted ceiling, this square-sided gazebo-style design throws partial shade onto an outdoor table and chairs.

An attractive gable in the centre of the roof is an eye-catching addition to this attached pergola, built at the rear of a house. Tinted polycarbonate sheeting shelters the west-facing wall from afternoon sun.

WORKING WITH NATURE

Large rocks or trees which at first appear to be in the way of your proposed pergola can be incorporated as important parts of the overall effect. Do not attempt to remove these so-called 'obstacles'; rather, use them to advantage by building around them. Aim to be both flexible and creative with your design, and add extra interest by incorporating unexpected angles and natural features.

CHOOSING A STYLE

There are two main types of pergola: attached and freestanding.

• Attached pergolas are fixed to a building for stability. An attached pergola, situated directly outside a house (often at the back door), is generally more useful than the freestanding alternative as it offers users easy access to amenities such as a kitchen and bathroom.

• Freestanding pergolas are usually set away from the house (often over an entry walkway) and stabilized with additional bracing.

Other variations include gazebos, arbours and walkways.

PREPARING PLANS

Sketch your chosen design, showing the relevant dimensions. Unless you are competent yourself, it is worth getting an architect or technical artist to draw up plans based on your design (more than one set is a good idea, as you may need to supply one to builders and timber merchants – plans can also become damaged easily on-site) and any specifications. These should provide a plan view, a side and end elevation view showing the necessary dimensions, and a cross-section view (drawn to a larger scale) setting out construction details.

Structures that are open on two or more sides are not subject to Building Regulations approval, whatever their size; however, you need to apply to your local council for planning permission if the pergola is to be more than 3000 mm high, or 4000 mm if it has a ridged roof, or is to be attached to a listed building.

To reduce the likelihood of making costly and wasteful errors, refer to the detailed drawings when calculating quantities and timber lengths and ordering materials for the project, and again at all stages during construction.

SITE PREPARATION

Once the design and location of your pergola are set, it is time to begin preparing the site. Concrete footings must be bedded firmly in the ground. If the soil is clayey or subjected to a lot of water, consider creating a rubble drain to divert run-off away from the structure. Any drain must be attached to either an absorption pit or a stormwater pipe that drains to the street – not on to your neighbour's property.

Level the site, if necessary, before construction begins. If excavating more than approximately 300 mm, seek advice on installing a retaining wall. Before starting work, reach an agreement with your suppliers on all plans and costs, as this type of wall can be expensive to create.

HINT

Many home building projects are never even started because the available site seems unsuitable for its intended use.

If preparation for your pergola involves the removal or deposit of large amounts of soil or gravel, hire an operator with a machine, such as an excavator, to do the heavy work for you, saving time and energy.

This applies equally to concreting, another daunting prospect for many weekend builders. When laying a slab, consider ordering a bulk delivery of ready-mix concrete from a reputable local contractor to reduce the workload and ensure your project remains achievable.

Although much smaller than the standard verandah-style pergola, this flat-roofed frame is a stylish addition to an entranceway. As a support for climbing plants, it can be used to provide light all-weather protection at the door.

CHOOSING TIMBER

Any timber used in a pergola faces exposure to all types of weather and can be subject to attack by insects. It must be able to withstand the test of time.

For detailed information on choosing timbers for outdoor structures such as pergolas, see Choosing material, pages 56–63 in the Building decks section.

Hardwoods are extremely heavy and difficult to handle and are not suited for use in overhead structures. They are best suited for use as posts.

More commonly used in pergola building are pressure-treated softwoods such as redwood and pine. Such softwoods are available from most timber merchants.

SEASONING

Using unseasoned timber in a project inevitably results in shrinking, warping or bowing as it dries, particularly in varieties of hardwood. Most hardwood is semi-seasoned when purchased as sawn timber for construction, making it easier to use. Much of the treated timber sold in Britain is seasoned.

When buying timber, watch for faults such as bowing or twisting. Lightly bowed or twisted timber can usually be pulled straight as it is fixed firmly into position, but badly disfigured pieces are often unusable.

PARTS OF A PERGOLA

Each pergola – whether freestanding or attached to another structure (such as a house) – consists of a series of standard parts.

FOOTINGS

A footing (normally poured from concrete into a temporary timber form box and allowed to harden in position) is placed in the ground to stabilize the structure. It must rest on a solid, compacted base capable of bearing the full load of the finished pergola safely without allowing any undue movement.

PIERS AND COLUMNS

The piers and columns, on which the wooden posts rest, are normally built of brick or constructed from reinforced concrete poured into a form tube. In high-wind areas, it is necessary to place a tie-down rod into each pier or column and embed it in the footing during the construction process.

As an alternative to traditional timber or metal posts, support the roof frame directly on brick columns constructed to the full height of the beam. Secure the beam with an iron hoop strap embedded in the brickwork and nailed to the timber. As a variation on this, you could construct a shorter column, finish it with a capping of tiles or sandstone and fix a concrete column or timber post to the top to extend it to the desired height.

Brick piers, columns and footings are free of council regulations, but check with the planning department if your house is a listed building.

TIMBER POSTS

Set round or square timber posts in concrete footings, or place them on top, secured in galvanized metal stirrups. You should either concrete each stirrup into the footing as it is being poured, or bolt it with masonry anchors to the surface once it has set.

STEEL POSTS

Embed steel posts of round or square section in a concrete footing, or bolt them down to the surface of the footing using masonry anchors. If you are using raw steel posts, protect them from corrosion by applying a galvanized coating. Drill a drainage hole near the bottom of each post to allow any excess water to escape.

FASCIA

A fascia board fixed over the ends of the rafters creates an attractive finish and provides a secure backing for the guttering.

LEDGER

In an attached pergola, a piece of timber known as the ledger is fixed to the wall of the house at the same height as that of the beam. The ledger acts as a second beam, tying the frame to the building and its solid foundation.

BEAMS

The overhead structure of a pergola consists of a frame of beams spanning the distance between the pergola posts. The beams of an attached pergola should run parallel to the house.

RAFTER

Each rafter spans the width of the pergola and is fixed from the beam to the ledger.

BATTENS

The roof covering is fixed to battens fastened on top of and at right angles to the rafters, parallel to the beam (and ledger when one is used).

BRACING

To help stabilize a pergola and prevent it swaying once construction has been completed, you should place angled timber or steel braces at appropriate points.

CHOOSING HARDWARE

Any pergola is only as strong as its fasteners and should therefore be built using good-quality hardware that will not corrode.

Generally, galvanized steel is the most durable material for fasteners and fittings that will be exposed to the weather.

Detailed information about hardware for outdoor projects is given in Hardware in the Building decks section, on pages 60–5.

Of particular relevance to building pergolas, special roofing screws are available in varieties ranging from stainless steel to hot-dipped galvanized metal, all of which come with neoprene washers.

Choose quality galvanised metal bolts, masonry anchors, joist hangers and roofing screws for an attached pergola such as this. Ensure any cut edges or drill holes are sealed to prevent corrosion.

A gable let into the centre of the roof interrupts a potentially uninteresting expanse of polycarbonate sheeting. The covering in this case is ideal, casting light shade on to the house wall and protecting the furniture from sun and rain.

Coverings and trims

Timber battens, lattice, awning cloth, sheeting – the variety of modern roofing materials suitable for pergola projects is broad. A roof covering should suit the general architectural style of the structure and its surrounds as well as its intended use.

ROOFING

Once the main structure is complete, either stop working altogether or prepare to add your choice of roof covering: timber battens, lattice, awning cloth or, to create a completely weatherproof area, polycarbonate, fibreglass or metal sheeting. Fix roof covering according to the manufacturer's instructions.

TIMBER BATTENS

Battens vary in size from 50 x 25 mm to more than 100 x 50 mm. The bigger battens generally look best on large pergolas, so keep the batten size in proportion to the job. You will find 70 x 35 mm treated pine suits most designs.

Fix the battens either flat or on edge at a 90 degree angle to the rafters (see the Attaching battens diagram, page 122). Space battens laid flat from 100 mm to 200 mm apart. The more closely the battens are positioned, the more shade is created, so adjust them to suit your needs. Battens fixed on edge should be spaced further apart (for example, at intervals of up to 300 mm).

Fix the battens securely to provide a sound base for the addition of roof

covering should you decide later to make your pergola into an all-weather outdoor area. Skew-nail two 75 x 3.5 mm galvanized lost-head nails through each batten into the top of the rafter.

LATTICE

Secure lattice directly to the tops of rafters with galvanized lost-head nails. This form of roof covering is ideal as a support for climbing plants or for providing filtered shade. Paint it, if desired, in coordinating colours to blend with the house.

AWNING CLOTH

Awning cloth is available in a range of colours to suit many decors, ranging from shades of green and blue to pink or brown.

Most manufacturers supply awning cloth in 30 per cent, 50 per cent and 70 per cent grades of shade (70 per cent coverage providing the heaviest protection from the sun). Awning cloth can be either woven or knitted, with the latter requiring edge treatment to prevent it fraying. Sew a hem on the cut edge or sandwich the cloth between the batten and a rafter. Fix all edges of

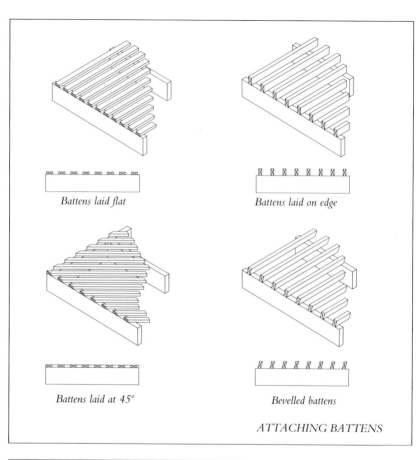

Battens laid flat

Battens laid on edge

Battens laid at 45°

Bevelled battens

ATTACHING BATTENS

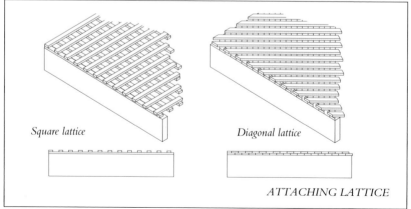

Square lattice

Diagonal lattice

ATTACHING LATTICE

the cloth to either battens or rafters for a long-lasting result.

POLYCARBONATE/FIBREGLASS SHEETING

Fibreglass roofing lets in light but gives a distorted view through the fibre reinforcement within each sheet. A popular contemporary choice is polycarbonate, which is free of fibres and therefore provides a clear outlook. Both types are available in a range of profiles and colours. Some filter out ultra-violet rays and are not recommended as coverings for plants. Ask at your local nursery or garden centre for advice.

Before securing fibreglass or polycarbonate sheeting, drill a

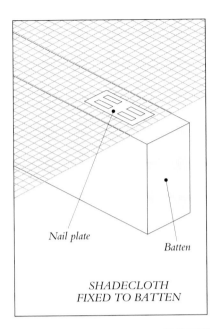

Nail plate

Batten

SHADECLOTH FIXED TO BATTEN

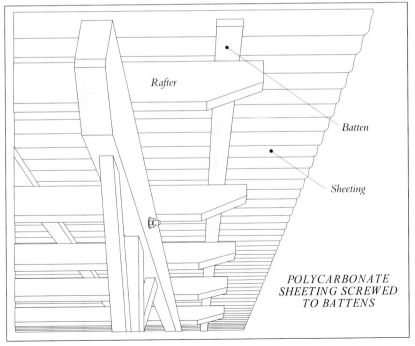

Rafter

Batten

Sheeting

POLYCARBONATE SHEETING SCREWED TO BATTENS

clearance hole through the sheet to allow for expansion and contraction. Fix it to the battens and install flashing and guttering in the same way as when using metal sheeting. To fix the sheets in place, use screws with neoprene washers. While self-drilling screws can be used on metal, they sometimes crack or split fibreglass or polycarbonate sheeting, and so are not suitable for such roofs.

METAL SHEETING

A metal roof cuts out the sun completely and is available in a choice of colours, the underside of which is usually an off-white shade.

To relieve the creaking noise caused by movement of the roofing as temperatures change, place foam rafter tape on top of the battens. Fix solid roof coverings to a 70 x 35 mm batten skew-nailed to the top of the rafters at a spacing recommended by the manufacturer (generally around 1 m apart).

Seal the gap between the house and the pergola with a shaped flashing. Use barge capping to finish the ends neatly, and install guttering with a downpipe to direct water run-off away from the structure.

FINISHING TOUCHES

To help your pergola blend with the existing style of your house, try to choose appropriate finishing touches.

SHAPED POSTS

Turned posts can be purchased in a variety of shapes and sizes, but these ready-made decorative options can prove expensive.

Transform plain square timber posts into distinctive features by cutting flutes or grooves in the faces and rounding off the square corners. Run these machine-routed trims the full height of the post, or stop short of both ends.

DADO MOULDS

To add interest to your pergola, fix shaped wooden or plastic mouldings, painted in a coordinating colour and mitre-joined at the corners, around each post approximately one quarter of the way down from the top.

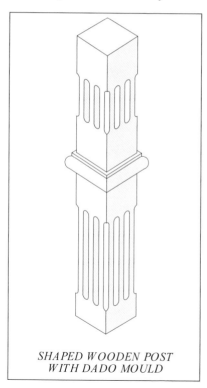

SHAPED WOODEN POST
WITH DADO MOULD

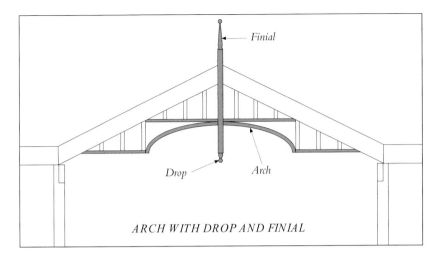

ARCH WITH DROP AND FINIAL

BRACKETS
Adding shaped brackets between the post and the beam is an easy way of giving your pergola a colonial-style look.

ARCHES
Place curved arches under the beams or in the ends of the gables to draw attention to an entry.

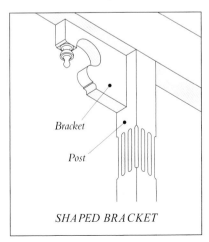

SHAPED BRACKET

DROPS AND FINIALS
Drops added under the ends of beams and finials positioned on the tops of gables are classically eyecatching and can be painted to match or contrast with the body of the structure.

PRIVACY SCREENS
Louvred or wooden lattice screens fixed between pairs of pergola posts increase privacy for the occupants, give added protection from the prevailing weather and create a feature wall. These screens also provide excellent support for climbing plants.

PLANTS
Hanging baskets and potted and climbing plants add life and colour to a pergola. Seek your local nursery expert's advice on the most appropriate deciduous or evergreen plants for your situation.

Estimating and ordering

Estimating the quantity of material required for each project is relatively simple using approved building plans as a guide. All calculations should be checked thoroughly with reference to a detailed list of components to ensure nothing is overlooked.

CALCULATING QUANTITIES
Working with your building plans as a guide, it is possible to estimate – not 'guesstimate' – the quantity of each material or item of hardware required for your pergola.

Set up a material list to ensure all the supplies and preliminaries are considered. Alternatively, simply work from the example provided on pages 128–9, ticking off each component in turn or expanding the model to create a chart with third and fourth columns headed 'quantity' and 'cost'. Working through a formal planning process on paper helps cost a project accurately to prevent initial overspending on unnecessary supplies that end up going to waste.

Refer to this list to ensure all essential aspects of the job are covered. Delete or add specific items as required to suit your particular circumstances.

Most timber merchants will assist you to order the correct quantities, grades and species of timber for your project if you show them your building plan.

When preparing a cutting guide, consider various options before selecting your timber length.

For example, if your project requires two 1800 mm lengths of timber but this is not available, do not buy 2400 mm pieces as 600 mm will be wasted from each. Instead, select a single 3600 mm length and cut it in half.

If you need numerous concrete footings to stabilize your pergola, or if a solid slab is required, you can order pre-mixed concrete to be delivered in bulk. This will save you from the heavy task of mixing your own. Check that clear vehicular access for the truck is available directly to your site.

HINT

Before beginning any form of excavation at your site, contact the relevant local authorities to request plans of underground pipes and cables running across your land. Make sure you consult your gas, water, electricity and telecommunications suppliers. Damaging these utilities not only exposes the home builder to the possibility of extreme physical danger but usually results in costly repair bills.

Work from an accurate builder's plan when preparing a materials list for a large attached pergola such as this. Careful planning eliminates wastage, minimizes cost and ensures adequate supplies are available as needed.

MATERIALS CHECKLIST	
MATERIAL	DESCRIPTION
PRELIMINARY PLANS	
Drawings/specifications	
Planning permission	If necessary; application form
FOOTINGS	
Formwork	
Excavation	Machinery hire or sub-contract
Concrete	Bag or ready-mix pump for difficult sites
Stirrups	Embedded or bolt-on
Drainage	Pipes, gravel
TIMBER	
Posts	Size, grade, type, length
Ledgers	
Beams	
Rafters	
Battens	
Fascia/barges	
Trimmers	
Bracing	
Props	Temporary bracing or props
Screens/screen frame or channel	Lattice, louvres
HARDWARE	
Galvanized post stirrups or brackets	One per post
Galvanized bolts or coach screws with washers	One per stirrup or bracket for attaching beam to post, ledger or wall
Masonry anchors	For attaching stirrups and ledgers to bricks or masonry
Roof covering	Corrugated iron, awning cloth, polycarbonate, fibreglass
Roofing screws, neoprene washers	For attaching roofing to battens
Flashing	

MATERIAL	DESCRIPTION
Downpipes	
Galvanized nails	Lost-head with plain or twist shanks, 75 x 3.5 mm for construction
Connectors	30 x 2.8 mm flat-head joist hangers, nail plates, cyclone straps
MISCELLANEOUS	
Paint	Stains, primers, filler and finish
Equipment hire	Power tools, compressor, nail gun, post-hole digger
Labour	
Landscaping	Retaining walls, plants, pavers, concrete
Incidental services	Delivery, waste disposal
TOTAL COST	

CHOOSING TOOLS

When assembling a basic building kit, choose good-quality tools designed to last for years. For best results, always buy recognized brands, and consult your local hardware stockist if you require additional advice.

When using power tools, always follow the instructions issued by the manufacturer.

Work in a well-lit area and ensure adequate ventilation is provided. Wear protective clothing to guard against eye damage and possible hearing loss.

Store your tools carefully in a secure, dry place. Using a tool rack or tool box helps protect them from incidental damage and allows you to see the range clearly. Alternatively, you can leave each tool in its original storage box.

BASIC TOOLS

- Handsaw
- Power saw
- Jigsaw
- Hammer and nail punch
- 25 mm chisel
- Builders square/combination square/sliding bevel
- Tape measure
- Marking gauge
- Power drill with assorted bits
- Spanner (in size to suit nuts)
- Stringline
- Shovel/spade/mattock
- Post-hole shovel
- Spirit level and water level
- Cramps
- Hand plane
- Router (optional)

Not all pergolas are additions to existing homes. This example, supported on sturdy concrete pillars, was incorporated into the original design. The eight rafters run horizontally from a ledger fixed to the brickwork under the eaves.

Building techniques

Most pergolas are attached directly to a house, increasing the stability of the structure and extending living space. Rafters are fixed to a wall-mounted ledger or attached to the fascia to avoid obstructing window or door openings directly under the eaves.

CHOOSING A METHOD

Usually, the connection of a pergola to a house is via a ledger bolted to an exterior wall. Rafters sit on top of the ledger or are fixed to the face with the aid of joist hangers.

Alternatively, rafters are fixed directly to the fascia, either with or without a ledger. The latter method is preferred where the tops of any window or door openings are directly under the eaves. A major advantage of this is the increased height of the finished pergola.

FIXING THE LEDGER

Fixing the ledger and rafters securely is important, as the structure must be able to withstand pressures from storms or wind, particularly if roofing is added. Attach the ledger directly to the face of brickwork with masonry anchors or fix it to a wall frame or fascia and rafter ends with coach screws. If the house is clad with weatherboards, remove a section to create a flat, even surface to accept the ledger. Place flashing directly above it to prevent water entering the house and causing damage.

When determining the height of a ledger – particularly if it is to be attached to a wall under the eaves – consider whether rafters, battens or roof coverings will be added above it, and leave room for them.

Wherever possible, position fastenings directly below alternate rafters on the pergola. Use an extra set of hands or temporary props to hold the work together during this process, as accuracy is important.

CONSTRUCTING BUILDING PROFILES

Use profiles to set out the stringlines for your project. Construct building profiles with pointed pegs and a horizontal cross-piece approximately 600 mm long. Ensure the pegs are strong enough to be driven deep into the ground to support the tightly stretched stringlines. Make sure the tops of the pegs are on a common horizontal plane.

INSTALLING FOOTINGS AND POSTS

Support the aerial structure on brick piers, concrete or steel columns or timber posts. Anchor the supports to the ground on concrete footings.

The spacing of the footings depends on the section size and grade of timber used for the beam. The size is influenced by the soil type and the style of post supporting the structure. The bottom of each footing must rest on stable ground, so remove tree roots and other obstacles.

Borrow or hire a post-hole shovel to dig the footing holes or, for larger jobs, hire a powered post-hole auger. (Obtain operating instructions from the hire company.) To use a post-hole shovel, hold the handles together and drive the blades into the ground several times to break up the packed soil. Spread the handles to hold the earth, then lift it out and dump the dirt far enough away from the excavation to prevent a cave-in.

When working with sandy soils that tend to fall into the hole as you dig, remove the top and bottom from a 5 gallon drum. Place the drum in position and dig through it, pushing the tube further into the excavation as you work. Leave the drum in place to act as a makeshift formwork when pouring wet concrete for the footing.

Alternatively, place a 100 mm high timber box over the hole. Centre the timber formwork and brace it temporarily to ensure it remains in place.

If you choose to install timber posts, the precise height of the footing is not important. Aim to have the footings levelled off at approximately 50 mm above the ground with the surrounding soil graded away to prevent water

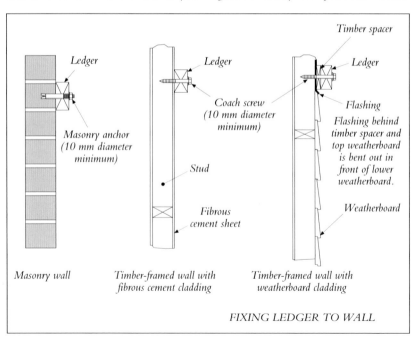

Ledger

Masonry anchor (10 mm diameter minimum)

Masonry wall

Ledger

Coach screw (10 mm diameter minimum)

Stud

Fibrous cement sheet

Timber-framed wall with fibrous cement cladding

Timber spacer

Ledger

Flashing

Flashing behind timber spacer and top weatherboard is bent out in front of lower weatherboard.

Weatherboard

Timber-framed wall with weatherboard cladding

FIXING LEDGER TO WALL

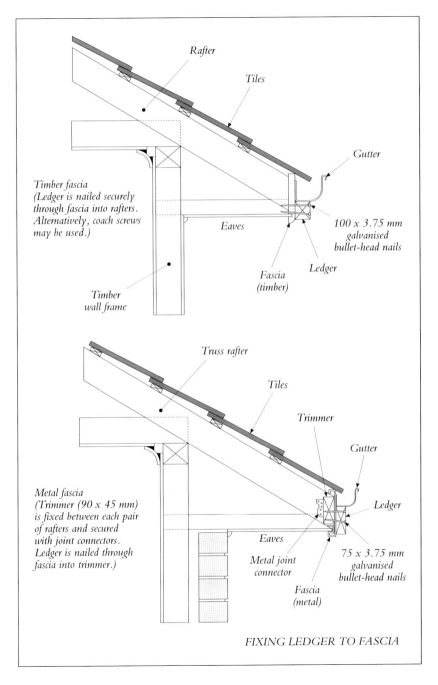

Rafter

Tiles

Gutter

Timber fascia
(Ledger is nailed securely
through fascia into rafters.
Alternatively, coach screws
may be used.)

Eaves

100 x 3.75 mm
galvanised
bullet-head nails

Fascia
(timber)

Ledger

Timber
wall frame

Truss rafter

Tiles

Trimmer

Gutter

Metal fascia
(Trimmer (90 x 45 mm)
is fixed between each pair
of rafters and secured
with joint connectors.
Ledger is nailed through
fascia into trimmer.)

Ledger

Eaves

Metal joint
connector

75 x 3.75 mm
galvanised
bullet-head nails

Fascia
(metal)

FIXING LEDGER TO FASCIA

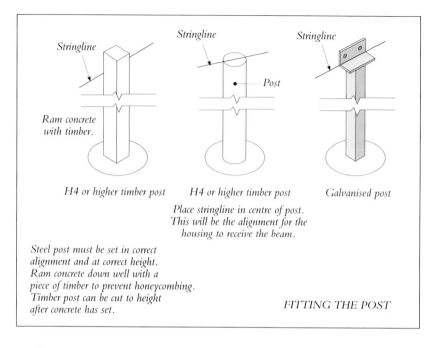

Stringline

Stringline

Stringline

Post

Ram concrete with timber.

H4 or higher timber post

H4 or higher timber post

Galvanised post

Place stringline in centre of post. This will be the alignment for the housing to receive the beam.

Steel post must be set in correct alignment and at correct height. Ram concrete down well with a piece of timber to prevent honeycombing. Timber post can be cut to height after concrete has set.

FITTING THE POST

pooling around the posts. (The tops of brick piers, on the other hand, must be below the beam at a level that accommodates an even number of brick courses, so the footing usually finishes below the ground.)

Mix the concrete until it is smooth enough to be poured yet stiff enough to hold the posts or stirrups upright while it sets.

Pour the mix into the form and use a piece of timber to ram it down well to prevent the formation of unwanted air pockets, known as 'honeycombing'. Honeycomb holds water, often causing posts and fittings to rot or rust.

Embed the stirrups, if required, in the wet concrete, aligning them carefully with the stringlines. (Fasten

bolt-down stirrups in position after the concrete has been left to set for approximately seven days.)

If using treated timber or steel posts, brace them temporarily while the concrete is poured and allowed to harden. Ensure the posts are perfectly plumb and in alignment, as there is no easy way to correct inaccuracies once the concrete is dry.

ATTACHING THE BEAM

To attach a beam to timber posts, cut a housing in the top of each post. Bolt the beam into position, securing it with two 12 mm diameter bolts. Make the housings no deeper than two-thirds the thickness of the post. Cut the housings with a power saw and clean them out with a chisel.

As an option, place beams on both sides of each post and block solidly in between. This enables smaller timber sections to be used. Keep both top edges in level alignment.

To create a housing in a round post, first measure the thickness of the beams on the tops and stretch a taut stringline from one post to the next. (See page 80, in the Building decks section.) The stringline represents the back of the housing.

Plumb a line down each side of the post and use a square piece of cardboard as a guide when marking the proposed height of the beam. Use a handsaw to make the crosscut for the housing and carefully remove the waste with a chisel.

Position the end joint of each beam directly over a post, and stagger them. For maximum strength, use a scarf joint to join beams end-to-end, or fix the beam to the top of a post.

ROOFING MATERIALS

The more conventional roofing materials for pergolas include battens, lattice, awning cloth, polycarbonate sheeting and fibreglass. However, there are many alternative materials that can be used to cover the structure for a distinctive effect, although they may not prove to be as durable or weatherproof.

REED OR BAMBOO
These inexpensive materials look charming and rustic but they have a limited lifespan. You can prolong their use by rolling them up and storing them inside during the winter months.

CANVAS
Heavy cotton duck gives some degree of rain protection, but it must be stretched taut across the pergola so that water won't collect on it.

VINES AND OTHER CLIMBING PLANTS
Grape vines, climbing plants and deciduous creepers have long been popular coverings for pergolas. They give shelter from the sun in summer and still allow the winter sunlight to penetrate.

A pergola needs to be sturdily constructed if heavy climbers such as wisteria or roses are to be grown over it. Don't wind roses around the posts of a pergola – roses need annual pruning, and cutting out twisted canes can become very difficult. Instead, use heavy guy wires attached to the piers or supporting posts, and tie the canes to these. Tie the plants loosely so the tie does not cut into the bark during the growing season. Where possible you should use twine or similar material that will break down with exposure to the elements.

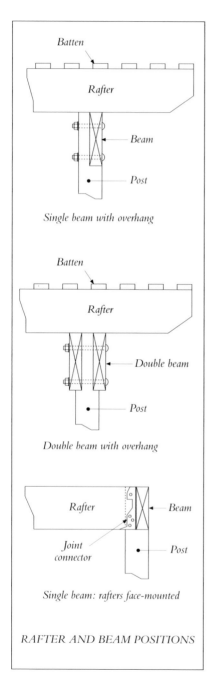

Single beam with overhang

Double beam with overhang

Single beam: rafters face-mounted

RAFTER AND BEAM POSITIONS

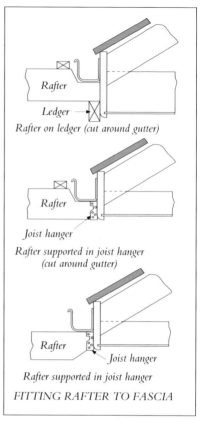

Rafter on ledger (cut around gutter)

*Rafter supported in joist hanger
(cut around gutter)*

Rafter supported in joist hanger

FITTING RAFTER TO FASCIA

If you choose to install a waterproof roof covering, ensure you provide a 1:40 fall to allow rainwater to run off. Direct run-off water along guttering to a downpipe.

ATTACHING RAFTERS

Rafters can sit on top of or against the face of a ledger and beam, or against the face of the ledger and over the beam. Where rafters fit against the face of a ledger and/or beam, use a joist hanger to strengthen the join.

Providing a rafter overhang of up to 600 mm beyond the beam reduces emphasis on the posts, which appear to be set back from the edge.

When using joist hangers, ensure the ledger and rafter are of equal size. Use an offcut of rafter material when positioning the hanger. Fix one side to the ledger with galvanized 30 x 2.8 mm clout nails (or an alternative recommended by the manufacturer). Allow a 10 mm gap between the wall and the end of any rafter fixed to the top of a ledger. If the rafters sit over a beam, square the ledger end of the two end rafters on the outside. Shape these ends if necessary (if they must fit neatly under the guttering). Measure the finished distance from the house to the outside edge of the beam, and add the width of the desired overhang. Shape the ends of the rafters to suit the design, ensuring any bows in the timber are placed to the top.

If the rafters are to fit between the ledger and the beam, cut them to the finished length. Apply a preservative and fit the ledger end of each rafter into its hanger. Fix the opposite side of each hanger to the ledger, then attach the hanger to the rafter.

Check that the posts are plumb and aligned. Skew-nail the other end of the rafter to the top of the beam, using a 75 x 3.5 mm galvanized nail. Strengthen the joint with galvanized steel joint connectors.

Measure the diagonals for square, and adjust them if necessary. Use a temporary brace, if desired, to hold the structure square. Complete the fixing of the two end rafters.

Cut the intermediate rafters to length, shaping the ends if required. Fix the intermediate rafters in place following the steps described above.

BRACING THE PERGOLA

The use of bracing need not detract from the appearance of a pergola. Conceal bracing behind lattice, battens or a trellis for a climbing vine. To create a colonial look, purchase pre-cut timber brackets from your local supplier.

A pergola fixed securely to a house (particularly in a corner) requires only minimal bracing. Fit an attached pergola with a pair of opposing braces running parallel to the house on each post. A simple 90 x 35 mm timber brace running at a 45 degree angle from the post to the beam is adequate in most situations. The angle can be allowed to vary slightly (by approximately 5 degrees).

Fix diagonal bracing to the tops of the rafters. Create half-laps in the centre, bolt each end with a 12 mm diameter bolt, and nail the bracing to the rafter, or use a steel angle framing brace in place of timber.

Once the braces are fixed permanently, remove any temporary bracing used to hold the structure during construction.

Fit pergolas in high-wind areas and freestanding models on stirrups with both types of braces: from post to beam and on top of the rafters.

Attached pergola

The most common pergolas are those attached to the fascia board of a house. This simple rectangular, flat-roofed pergola – measuring 3300 x 3900 mm – is fixed to the fascia by a ledger and supported by timber posts with bolt-down stirrups.

```
TOOLS
─────────────────────
• Basic tool kit (see page 129)
```

quantities, pages 126–9). Specific requirements for this project are listed below.

PREPARATION
1 Referring to your detailed plans, estimate the quantities required and order your materials (see Calculating

2 With the timber laid out on the ground, apply one or two coats of the paint or stain of your desired colour before construction begins.

MATERIALS★

PART	TIMBER	LENGTH	No.
Post	90 x 90 mm treated pine (C24, 4A)	2400 mm	2
Beam	190 x 45 mm treated pine (C24, 4A)	3900 mm	1
Rafter	140 x 45 mm treated pine (C24, 4A)	3300 mm	7
Batten	70 x 35 mm treated pine (C24, 4A)	3900 mm	5
Ledger	70 x 45 mm treated pine (C24, 4A)	3900 mm	1
Trimmer	90 x 45 mm treated pine (C24, 4A)	3900 mm	1
Bracing	90 x 35 mm treated pine (C24, 4A)	2400 mm	1
Form box	90 x 19 mm offcuts	300 mm	8

OTHER: Two 40 kg bags of concrete; two galvanized stirrup post supports; eight 125 x 12 mm galvanized cup-head nuts and bolts with washers; twenty-one galvanized joint connectors (to suit); seven 90 x 45 mm galvanized joist hangers; 5 kg of 75 x 3.75 mm galvanized lost-head nails; four 75 x 10 mm galvanized masonry anchors; five 3300 mm sheets of 760 mm cover corrugated polycarbonate sheeting; one hundred 75 mm galvanized roofing screws with washers; 20 m roll of 25 mm rafter tape; timber preservative; stain or paint, primer and undercoat

★ Finished size: 3300 x 3900 mm. The timber lengths given are for a project similar to that shown opposite. Adapt these requirements to suit your needs.

Attached to the house, this flat-roofed pergola extends the occupants' living space well into the garden. A ledger fixed to a trimmer behind the fascia supports the rafters, and posts in galvanized metal stirrups hold the beam.

Be prepared to touch up later around the joints and on the cut ends.

FIXING THE LEDGER

3 Determine the length of the ledger by marking the outside face of each end rafter directly on to the fascia.

4 Place trimmers behind the metal fascia to create a solid surface. Slide the bottom row of roof tiles up to gain access. Measure and cut a trimmer to fit between each pair of rafters. Nail through the rafters into the ends of each trimmer with two 75 mm lost-head nails. Fix a joint connector behind the trimmer and on to the side of the rafter for added strength. Replace the tiles.

5 Cut the ledger to length and fix it to the fascia with lost-head nails driven through the fascia board.

DETERMINING THE POST POSITIONS

6 Using a plumb bob, plumb a line from each end of the ledger to the ground. Drive temporary pegs into the ground at these points, then replumb to the top of each peg. Drive nails at these positions, leaving them protruding slightly from the pegs. Tie a stringline to each nail.

7 To ensure your set-out is as close as possible to square, place a builders square on the ground against the house wall and the peg. From the top of the peg, measure out the required distance for the posts, then sight back along the edge of the square. Place temporary corner pegs in the ground at these points. Erect two profiles about 600 mm outside each corner peg. Pull a stringline parallel to the house to

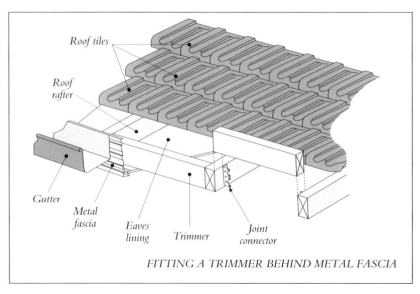

Roof tiles

Roof rafter

Gutter

Metal fascia

Eaves lining

Trimmer

Joint connector

FITTING A TRIMMER BEHIND METAL FASCIA

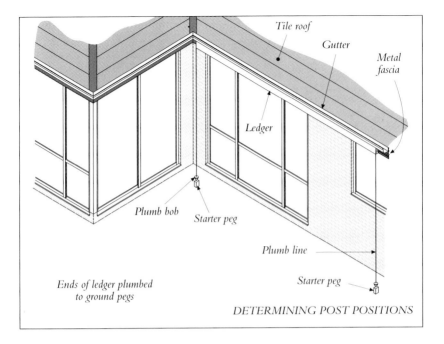

Tile roof

Gutter

Metal fascia

Ledger

Plumb bob

Starter peg

Plumb line

Starter peg

Ends of ledger plumbed
to ground pegs

DETERMINING POST POSITIONS

represent the outside face of the posts and beam, passing over the tops of the temporary corner pegs.

8 From the original pegs under the ledger, pull a separate stringline to the second set of profiles, passing over the temporary corner pegs and intersecting the first stringline.

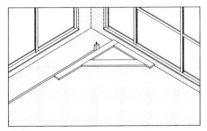

7 To ensure the set-out is square, place a builders square on the ground against the house wall and the peg.

9 Check the set-out for parallel and measure the diagonals for square. Adjust the stringlines.

10 The posts are set 300 mm in from the outside rafters. Measure this distance along the stringline parallel to the house, and mark the required footing holes with temporary pegs.

POURING THE FOOTINGS

11 Once the set-out has been checked, tack a nail beside the stringline into the top of each profile. These nails represent the permanent positions of the stringlines and are used later as anchors for the string. Situate the footings so they extend beyond this line. Ensure the post will sit in the centre of each footing.

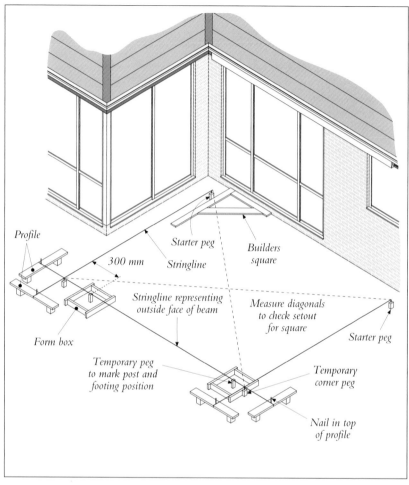

Profile

300 mm

Starter peg

Stringline

Builders
square

Stringline representing
outside face of beam

Form box

Measure diagonals
to check setout
for square

Starter peg

Temporary peg
to mark post and
footing position

Temporary
corner peg

Nail in top
of profile

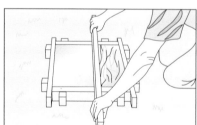

13 Place a form box in position and
pour in the concrete. Pull a straight
edge across the top.

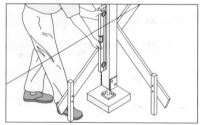

16 Stand the posts in the stirrups and
brace them temporarily. Check for
plumb and nail them into place.

12 Place a 300 x 300 mm form box in the required position under the stringline. Scratch the outline of the box on the ground to mark the location of the footing. Remove the stringlines and box and dig the 300 x 300 mm footings to 450 mm deep.

13 Place the form box in position, ensuring it is level, and pour in the concrete. Pull a straight edge across the top. Allow the concrete to set, remove the form box, and fill around the hole with soil.

14 Replace the stringlines, securing them to the nails in the tops of the profiles. Using a spirit level, plumb a line down from the stringline to the top of each footing and place a mark on the concrete to represent the outside face of each post.

ERECTING THE POSTS

15 Cut a length of post material long enough to reach from the top of the footing to the stringlines. Secure it temporarily with nails in a stirrup. Position this on top of each footing, with the outside face of the post plumb with the stringline. Mark the bolt holes at the top of each footing and drill with a tungsten-tipped masonry drill bit. Make each hole slightly deeper than the length of the fastener. Bolt the stirrups down firmly with masonry anchors.

16 Stand the posts in the metal stirrups and brace them. Check for vertical. Nail the post temporarily into the stirrup.

ATTACHING THE BEAM

17 With a water level and pencil, transfer the position of the bottom of the ledger to each post to represent the top of the beam.

18 As heights sometimes vary, number each post and corresponding stirrup to allow for easy reassembly. Mark crosses on the sides where the beam will be housed. Remove each post from its stirrup and place it on saw stools. Cut a housing in the top of each post to support the beam.

19 Re-erect the posts and brace them, checking for vertical.

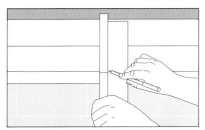

17 *With a water level and pencil, transfer the position of the bottom of the ledger to each post.*

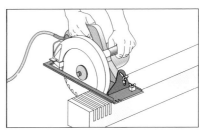

18 *Place each post on saw stools and cut a housing in the top to support the beam.*

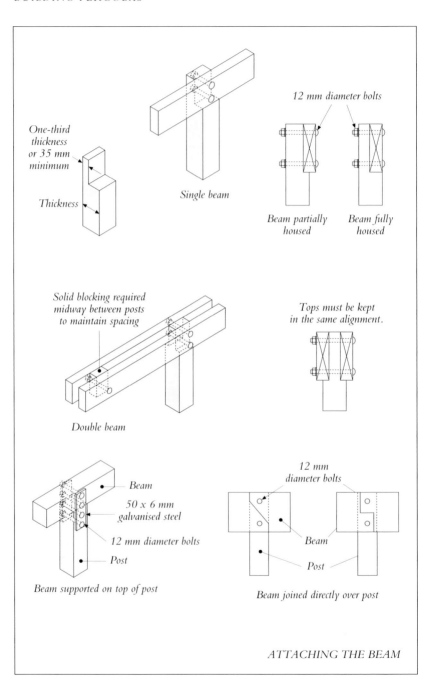

One-third
thickness
or 35 mm
minimum

Thickness

Single beam

12 mm diameter bolts

Beam partially
housed

Beam fully
housed

Solid blocking required
midway between posts
to maintain spacing

Tops must be kept
in the same alignment.

Double beam

Beam

50 x 6 mm
galvanised steel

12 mm diameter bolts

Post

Beam supported on top of post

12 mm
diameter bolts

Beam

Post

Beam joined directly over post

ATTACHING THE BEAM

20 The beam overhangs the posts by 450 mm and has a 45 degree splay cut on its bottom edge. Trim and shape the beam. Dress with a hand plane. Place the beam in its housings and clamp it into position. Drill two holes through the beam and posts and insert 12 mm diameter cup-head bolts with nuts.

ATTACHING THE RAFTERS
21 The rafters, with a 30 degree splay and a 450 mm overhang, are cut around the guttering of the house. Position the end rafters 300 mm outside the corner posts.

22 Ensure any bows face towards the top of the pergola. Cut the rafters to length, then shape them. Secure one side of the joist hanger to the ledger and insert the rafter. Attach the remaining side to the ledger and secure the rafter to the hanger. Skew-nail the remaining end to the top of the beam with 75 x 3.5 mm lost-head nails.

23 Measure the distance between the two outside rafters and divide this by the spacing required. This project uses five intermediate rafters positioned 650 mm apart.

24 Mark the rafter positions on the ledger and the top edge of the beam. Cut and shape the intermediate rafters. Secure them with joist hangers and skew-nail as described for the outside rafters.

BRACING THE BEAM
25 Trim four 450 mm braces (two per post) at a 45 degree angle on each end to fit under the beam and against the post. Nail through the edge of the brace into the beam and post, using 75 mm galvanized lost-head nails. Skew-nail through each face of the brace into the beam and post. Remove any makeshift bracing.

ATTACHING THE BATTENS
26 Cut the ends of the battens flush with the faces of the outside rafters. Fix the first batten at a 90 degree angle, 25 mm out from the guttering. Use two 75 mm galvanized lost-head nails driven through the top of each rafter.

23 Measure the distance between the two outside rafters and divide this by the spacing required.

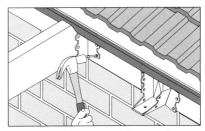

24 Secure the intermediate rafters to the ledger with joist hangers and skew-nail to the beam.

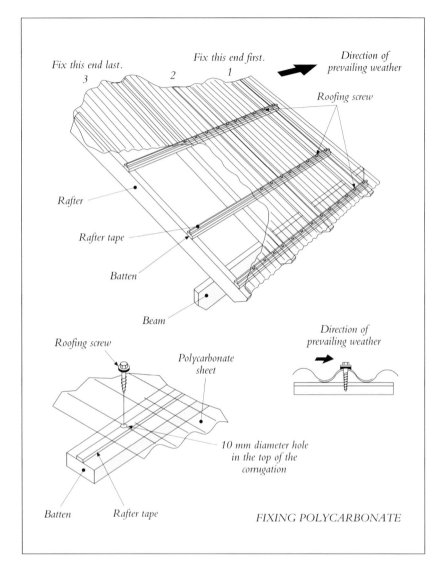

Fix this end last.
3

Fix this end first.
2   1

Direction of
prevailing weather

Roofing screw

Rafter

Rafter tape

Batten

Beam

Roofing screw

Polycarbonate
sheet

Direction of
prevailing weather

10 mm diameter hole
in the top of the
corrugation

Batten   Rafter tape

FIXING POLYCARBONATE

27 Position the outside batten 75 mm in from the ends of the rafters and fix it securely.

28 In this project, three intermediate battens are used to support the polycarbonate roofing sheets. Determine their spacing by dividing the distance between the outside battens by the number of intermediate battens. Place the battens approximately 900 mm apart

and fix them to the rafters with lost-head nails.

ATTACHING THE POLYCARBONATE

29 To minimize noise caused by the expansion and contraction of polycarbonate sheeting, place rafter tape on top of each batten before fixing the roofing in place.

30 Using a panel saw, cut the polycarbonate sheeting to length, allowing an overhang of 25 mm on the house side and 100 mm past the outside batten.

31 Determine the direction of the prevailing winds and lay the sheets to prevent wind or rain blowing under the overlaps. Position the first sheet flush with the ends of the battens.

32 Working one sheet at a time, drill a 10 mm hole through the top of the first corrugation in line with the centre of the batten. Secure the sheeting with a roofing screw. Ensure the screw passes through the centre of the hole and is square to

the top of the batten. Use only normal pressure when tightening the screws, as overtightening can distort or crack the sheet and restrict necessary movement.

33 Adjust the sheet to ensure it is square. Drill a hole in the other end and secure that, too, then continue fixing the edge. Drill through the top of every second corrugation and screw it to the batten, leaving room to overlap the next sheet.

34 Place the second sheet in position with an overlap of one-and-a-half corrugations. Drill through both sheets and screw them down. Measure periodically to check for square, and adjust the sheeting as necessary. Continue to work across the roof until the polycarbonate sheeting is fully fastened.

35 Fit flashing, capping or guttering as required.

FINISHING
36 Touch up the paintwork to guard against weathering.

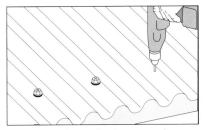

33 Drill through the top of every second corrugation and screw the roofing sheet to the batten.

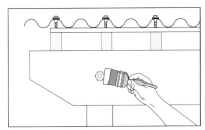

36 Touch up the paintwork as required to guard against weathering where raw timber is exposed.

Before erecting a pitched roof such as this, remember that additional rainfall running off the pergola might overwhelm the existing gutter and downpipe. Here, access for clearing fallen debris from the gutter is also difficult.

Gabled pergola

This gabled pergola measures 3300 x 6600 mm. The outside is supported on timber posts and incorporates collar ties for stability. The roof covering is polycarbonate sheeting, with guttering and a downpipe attached to the beam.

ESTIMATING YOUR MATERIALS

1 Referring to your detailed plans, order supplies for this project (see Calculating quantities, pages 126–9).

PREPARATION

2 Follow the steps described for the attached pergola (see Fixing the ledger, Determining the post positions, Pouring the footings, Erecting the posts and Attaching the beam, pages 140–5).

CREATING THE GABLE

3 With the ledger and beam in place and the posts braced temporarily, measure the distance between the ledger and beam. This measurement is the width of the pergola, which when finished has a central ridge board at the apex with equal rafters running down both sides.

Pitched roofs are constructed at an angle of between 22.5 degrees and 30 degrees. This roof is pitched at 26.5 degrees, which means the rise equals one-quarter of the span.

4 Divide the distance between the ledger and the beam by two and subtract half the ridge thickness.

This figure is the horizontal span of the rafter.

(Span ÷ 2) – half ridge thickness
= (3300 mm ÷ 2) – 25mm
= 1650 mm – 25 mm = 1625 mm

5 To calculate the rise, divide that figure by two.

1625 mm ÷ 2 = 812.5 mm (813 mm rounded off)

MARKING OUT THE RAFTER

6 To gauge the length of each rafter, use a builders square and rafter buttons to set up a pitch template. Calculate this as the horizontal span of the rafter divided by (say) five.

1625 mm ÷ 5 = 325 mm

7 Set one button 325 mm along the blade of the builders square. Set the other rafter button half this measurement (162.5 mm) along the stock of the square.

8 Trace the pitch template along the straightest rafter piece six times.

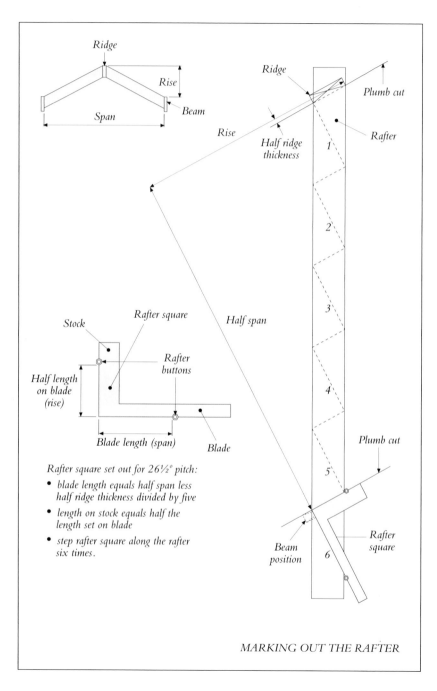

Ridge

Rise

Span

Beam

Ridge

Plumb cut

Rafter

Rise

Half ridge
thickness

1

2

3

Half span

4

Plumb cut

5

Beam
position

6

Rafter
square

Stock

Rafter square

Rafter
buttons

Half length
on blade
(rise)

Blade length (span)

Blade

Rafter square set out for 26½° pitch:

- blade length equals half span less
  half ridge thickness divided by five
- length on stock equals half the
  length set on blade
- step rafter square along the rafter
  six times.

MARKING OUT THE RAFTER

Cut the rafter on the first and last lines made by the stock of the square (see the Marking out the rafter diagram, opposite). Cut one rafter, then lay it on another and trace the outline. Keep any bows to the top. On a third length of timber, trace the rafter outline again, but do not cut it out. Position the first two rafters to check carefully for fit, making adjustments as required. Transfer any corrections on to the third rafter.

ERECTING THE GABLE

9 Cut the ridge board to length at 6600 mm. To check your angles and sizes, lay a pair of rafters flat on the ground with an offcut of ridge material between them. Measure the span distance at the ends of the rafters to ensure its accuracy.

10 Cut the ledger end of the rafter to fit around the guttering. Make straight cuts with a power saw or, for a neater fit, shape the cuts with a template and jigsaw. Make a template for the shape of the gutter from a piece of scrap ply or other material. Trace this on to the bottom end of one rafter and cut around it carefully with a jigsaw.

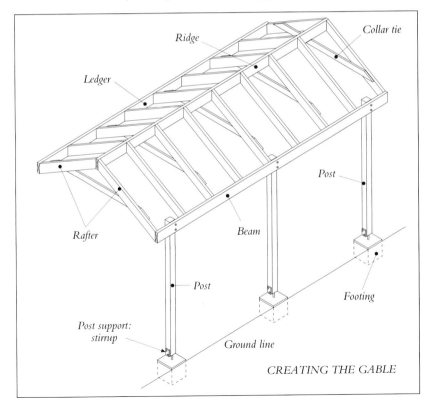

Ridge

Collar tie

Ledger

Post

Rafter

Beam

Post

Footing

Post support: stirrup

Ground line

CREATING THE GABLE

MATERIALS★

Part	Timber	Length	No.
Post	100 x 100 mm sawn pine (C16)	2400 mm	3
Beam	200 x 50 mm sawn pine (C16)	6600 mm	1
Rafter	150 x 50 mm sawn pine (C16)	2100 mm	24
Batten	75 x 50 mm sawn pine (C16)	6600 mm	8
Ledger	150 x 50 mm sawn pine (C16)	6600 mm	1
Ridge	150 x 50 mm sawn pine (C16)	6600 mm	1
Collar tie	150 x 50 mm sawn pine (C16)	2100 mm	6
Collar tie	75 x 50 mm batten sawn pine	2100 mm	1
Form box	90 x 19 mm offcuts	300 mm	12
Bottom rail	70 x 45 mm treated pine (C24)	2100 mm	1
Baluster	45 x 45 mm treated pine (C24)	900 mm	5
Finial	70 x 70 mm treated pine (C24)	1200 mm	1
Bracket	150 x 50 mm sawn pine (C16) offcuts	450 mm	2

OTHER: Three 40 kg bags of concrete; three galvanized stirrup post supports; twenty-four 125 x 12 mm galvanized cup-head nuts and bolts with washers; 10 kg of 75 x 3.75 mm galvanized lost-head nails; six 75 x 10 mm galvanized masonry anchors; eighteen 2100 mm sheets of 760 mm cover corrugated polycarbonate sheeting; two hundred 75 mm galvanized roofing screws with washers; 40 m roll of 25 mm rafter tape; four 2100 mm lengths of 150 x 75 mm steel barge capping; 3600 mm length of 300 mm steel ridge capping; clear silicone sealant; paint, primer and undercoat

★ Finished size: 3300 x 6600 mm. The timber lengths given are for the project pictured on page 148. Adapt these requirements to suit your own needs.

ATTACHING THE RAFTERS

11 Choose one end of the pergola as a starting point. You will need two ladders and a second person to help you when attempting this step. While one person stands on a ladder and holds the ridge end of the rafter and a scrap of ridge in place, the other should secure the ledger end by skew-nailing through the face into the ledger with two 75 x 3.75 mm galvanized lost-head nails. Repeat this process on the beam side, nailing the scrap piece of ridge temporarily between the rafters to maintain the required angle. Do not drive this nail in too far, as it must be removed once the ridge is in place. Check for fit and adjust the third rafter as required.

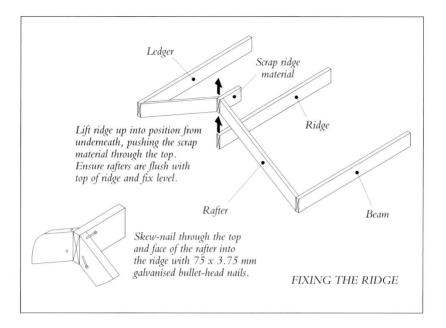

Ledger

Scrap ridge material

Lift ridge up into position from underneath, pushing the scrap material through the top. Ensure rafters are flush with top of ridge and fix level.

Ridge

Rafter

Beam

Skew-nail through the top and face of the rafter into the ridge with 75 x 3.75 mm galvanised bullet-head nails.

FIXING THE RIDGE

12 Cut the third rafter to length. This becomes the template for the rest of the rafters. Ensuring all bows will be at the top of the rafters, mark out the remaining rafters. As sawn timber can vary in width by as much as 5 mm or more, keep the tops in alignment so any variations are underneath. Cut the rafters to length. Shape half the rafters to fit around

12 Use a ply template to shape half the rafters to fit around the roof gutter on the house.

the gutter. Use the ply guttering template when tracing the outline on to the ledger ends of these rafters, then cut with a jigsaw. Position another pair of rafters at the opposite end of the pergola and fix as described above.

FIXING THE RIDGE

13 Have some temporary braces on hand to steady the ridge while you work. With one person at either end of the ridge, lift it up into position between the rafters, pushing the scrap ridge material through the top. Ensure the rafters are flush with the top and ends of the ridge. Check the ridge for level and fix it permanently in place by skew-nailing through the top and sides of each rafter into the ridge. Sight across one end of the

pergola, ensuring the end of the beam, the ridge and the ledger are in alignment. Fix temporary bracing to maintain this position.

FIXING THE INTERMEDIATE RAFTERS

14 Measuring from one end of the pergola, mark even spacings on the ledger, ridge and beam. Fix the rafters in pairs of one ledger rafter and one beam rafter to prevent the ridge and beam bowing, and skew-nail into position.

POSITIONING COLLAR TIES

15 Install collar ties two-thirds of the way down alternate pairs of rafters (see the Creating the gable diagram, page 151). Measure each rafter from the top of the ridge to the top of the beam. Mark the two-thirds point, calculated by multiplying the rafter length by two-thirds. In this case, each rafter measures 1817 mm.

1817 mm x 0.667 = 1211.939 mm (1212 mm rounded off)

Position the bottom of the collar tie on the mark and clamp it in place.

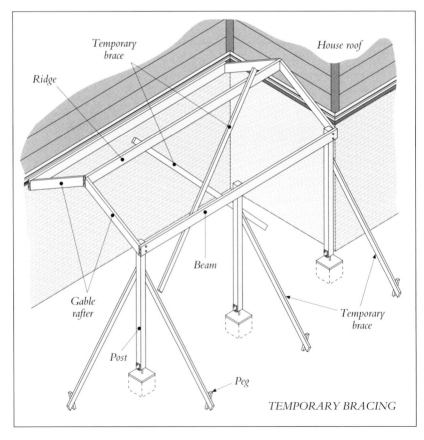

TEMPORARY BRACING

Check for level and adjust as required. Mark the rafter angle with a pencil on the face of the collar tie. Remove it and cut the angle with a power saw. Re-position and clamp it, checking for level. Drill a 12 mm hole through the collar tie and rafter and secure it with a cup-head bolt, nut and washer at each end.

FIXING THE BATTENS

16 Let the battens in or nail them to the tops of the rafters. In this example, the battens are let in with a power saw and chisel. To determine the positions and ensure they are straight, use a stringline. On one side of the pergola, mark 100 mm from the bottom on both end rafters. Place a nail in the top of each rafter at this point and pull a stringline between them. Using a square, mark the top of each rafter, along the stringline. This identifies the bottom edge of the batten. Use an offcut of batten material to gauge the width of the housing (about 75 mm) in each rafter and mark it with a pencil.

17 Fix the ridge capping to the top batten. As the capping used here is 300 mm wide, measure 150 mm down each side from the centre of the ridge. The bottom edge of the batten rests here. As described above, use a stringline and batten offcut to mark the housings. Place the intermediate battens evenly between the top and bottom battens and set them out in the same manner. Repeat on the other side of the roof.

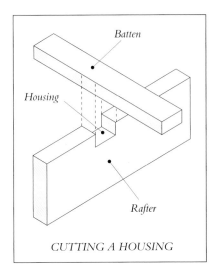

CUTTING A HOUSING

CUTTING THE HOUSINGS

18 Set a power saw to a depth to suit the battens. (In this case, 50 mm is appropriate.) Make several cuts in the housing to make chiselling easy. Chisel the waste away from both sides and level the bottom of each housing. Use the batten offcut to check for fit and adjust as required.

19 Cut the battens to length and position them in the housings. Secure each batten with two

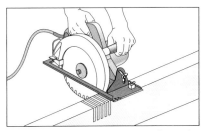

18 Make several cuts within the housing to make chiselling easy. Chisel the waste away from the sides.

75 x 3.75 mm galvanized lost-head nails driven from the batten into the rafter.

ATTACHING THE ROOF

20 The roof covering for this pergola is basically the same as that described for the attached structure (see Attaching the polycarbonate, page 147), and it is fixed in a similar manner. However, this pergola has the addition of metal barge and ridge capping, so do not secure the outside edges of the end sheets and the ridge ends of all sheets until the cappings are in place. Fill the gable end nearest the house with polycarbonate laid vertically to provide additional weatherproofing. The polycarbonate sheeting hangs down into the gutter by 25 mm. Provide a flat base for its attachment by ensuring the thickness of the collar ties on the end pair of rafters increases by the thickness of a rafter. To do this, place a batten on the face of the collar tie between the rafters. All temporary bracing can now be removed.

FIXING THE METAL CAPPINGS

21 Cut barge capping to cover the gap between the polycarbonate and the rafter faces at each end. Shape the lower end to fit around the guttering and against the ledger. Plumb-cut the other end 5 mm longer than the centre line of the ridge. On the opposite side of the barge capping, create a plumb cut at each end to match the ridge and beam.

22 Position the capping over the polycarbonate sheeting and push firmly against the face of the rafters. Drill through the top face and the polycarbonate and secure both to the battens with roofing screws. Do not fix to the ridge batten until the ridge capping is in place.

23 Place the second capping over the face and secure it in the same manner. Seal the overlapping join with clear silicone. Position ridge capping on top of the ridge and drill through it, then screw firmly through the polycarbonate into the ridge batten. Use two pieces to make up the required length. Fix the first capping flush with the outside face of the barge capping. Cut the second piece of ridge capping to length, allowing a 100 mm overlap. Seal the overlapping join with clear silicone and fix as before.

GABLE DECORATION

24 The bottom rail supports the balusters and brackets. Position it midway down the end of the gable. Bevel the ends to match the angle of the rafters. Before securing the bottom rail, check it for level. Fix it in place with two 75 mm lost-head nails driven into the bottom of each rafter end.

25 Fix a 150 mm offcut of batten vertically to the face of the end collar tie as a flat backing for the finial. Position the finial over the face of the gable end so the square section

protrudes an equal distance above the ridge and below the bottom rail. Check the finial for plumb and clamp it into position. Secure the finial to the ridge, collar-tie block and bottom rail. Use two 75 mm lost-head nails at each joint.

26 To determine the spacing between the balusters, measure the distance between the finial and the end of the bottom rail and divide it by the number of spaces required. This pergola project uses five balusters on each side of the finial, so divide the distance in this case by six. Working from the centre towards the outside, place a baluster on the bottom rail and hold it in position against the rafter. Check for vertical using a spirit level, and scribe a mark on the back to match the angle of the rafter. Cut the baluster to length.

Using 75 mm lost-head nails, fix it into position by nailing through the bottom rail into the baluster and skew-nailing through the top of the baluster into the rafter. Measure the distance to the next baluster and repeat this step.

27 For a more attractive look below the bottom rail, shape brackets from offcuts of rafter material and nail them in place.

FINISHING

28 Place guttering on the beam to divert rainwater away from the pergola. Add a downpipe connected to a stormwater drain.

29 Complete the paintwork as desired. This pergola is finished with two coats of external acrylic paint in contrasting colours.

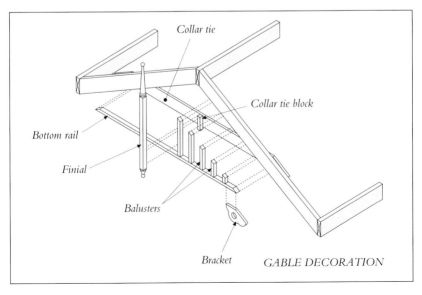

Collar tie

Collar tie block

Bottom rail

Finial

Balusters

Bracket

GABLE DECORATION

Freestanding walkway

This versatile design can be an arbour to support climbing plants, a grand garden entrance, an entertaining area or even a carport. It is supported on treated pine posts embedded in concrete and covered by lattice.

ESTIMATING YOUR MATERIALS

1 Referring to your detailed plans, estimate your material requirements and place the order (see Calculating quantities, pages 126–9).

PAINTING THE TIMBER

2 Remember to apply one or two coats of paint or stain in your desired colour before beginning to construct the pergola. It is easier to paint loose pieces of timber on the ground than when the structure is standing upright. Once the assembly is complete, you can touch up the joints and around the cut ends.

TOOLS

- Basic tool kit (see page 129)

PREPARATION

3 Determine a building line for the front of the walkway. Lay a piece of timber across the path to represent the starting line. The path in this project measures 600 mm wide and has a 300 mm allowance for the post positions at each side. To determine the front positions, measure 300 mm to each side of the path on the building line. Place wooden pegs temporarily in the ground at these points to represent the outside faces

MATERIALS*

PART	TIMBER	LENGTH	NO.
Post	90 x 90 mm treated pine (C24, 4A)	3000 mm	4
Beam	140 x 45 mm treated pine (C24, 3)	3000 mm	2
Rafter	140 x 45 mm treated pine (C24, 3)	2100 mm	4

OTHER: Eight 125 x 12 mm galvanized cup-head nuts and bolts with washers; 2 kg of 75 x 3.75 mm galvanized lost-head nails; stain or paint, primer and undercoat; approximately two buckets of coarse gravel; concrete; timber preservative; lattice (optional)

* Finished size: 2400 x 1200 mm (footprint) by 2100 mm high. The timber lengths given above are for the project pictured on page 159. Adapt these requirements to suit your own needs.

Clothed in wisteria and climbing roses, this simple white wooden structure is perfectly at home in its garden setting. Supported by four posts, it is quick to build, with four rafters resting on parallel beams.

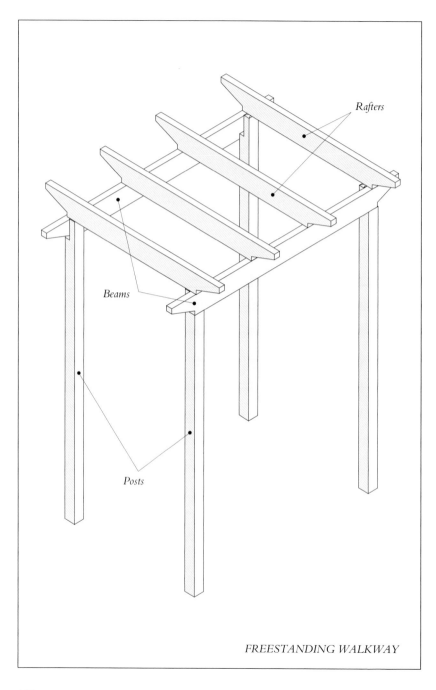

Rafters

Beams

Posts

FREESTANDING WALKWAY

of the posts. Just outside each peg, erect a building profile across the corner, at an angle of approximately 45 degrees. Insert a nail in the top of each profile and stretch a stringline between the two, securing it to create a building line.

4 Place a spirit level on top of the temporary corner pegs and plumb to the stringline. Wrap masking tape around the string, then draw with a pencil on to the taped section where the plumb line crosses to create a clearly visible mark.

5 From the temporary corner pegs, measure 2400 mm along the path and drive in a second set of corner pegs. Erect another pair of profiles as described previously. Pull a stringline down one side of the path, making sure it passes over the masking tape mark. Drive in an additional nail and secure the stringline. Repeat this step on the other side of the path. Measure the distance between the stringlines at two points to ensure they are parallel, adjusting them as required.

6 Working from the second set of temporary corner pegs, plumb up to the stringline and mark it clearly. Stretch another stringline across the path from one profile to the other, passing over the two marks. Measure the diagonals between the intersecting stringlines to check that they are equal and that, therfore, the project is square. Once the set-out is

---

HINT

Protect timber from insect and water damage by applying a coat of preservative to all joints prior to fixing.

---

correct, remove the stringlines to provide easy access while digging the footings.

DIGGING THE FOOTINGS

7 As the stringline represents the outside face of the post, the footing must extend beyond this line. The post sits in the centre of each footing. Scratch the outline of the footing on the ground to mark the position of the hole and dig each footing 300 x 300 mm and to a depth of 550 mm.

8 Add a 100 mm layer of coarse gravel to the bottom of each hole to aid drainage, particularly in areas with heavy clay-based soil.

9 Replace the stringlines and secure them tightly to the nails in the tops of the profiles.

ERECTING POSTS

10 Stand each post carefully in its hole, ensuring it is vertical and in line

---

HINT

Use stainless steel fasteners and fittings in highly corrosive conditions (such as in areas with spray from salt water).

When designing a freestanding pergola as a companion to an existing structure (such as this house), consider its overall dimensions. To create a pleasing scene, make sure its scale is in keeping with that of the original building.

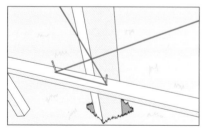

10 Stand each post carefully in its hole, ensuring it is vertical and in line with the intersecting stringlines.

with the intersecting stringlines. Work with posts slightly longer than required, trimming any excess away later.

11 Brace them temporarily and recheck for vertical. Mix cement and sharp sand with water. to form concrete to the consistency of stiff paste, then pour it into the hole.

Ram the wet concrete down well to remove any air bubbles trapped in the mixture and ensure the post is held firmly. Before beginning construction, allow the concrete to set for at least seven days and up to a fortnight.

FIXING THE BEAMS

12 In this project, the beams run parallel to the path at a height of 2100 mm. Beginning with those – if any – that stand on slightly higher ground, measure up from the bottom of each post and square a line around all four sides. Use a spirit level, a straight edge and a pencil to transfer the beam marks to the remaining three posts.

13 Place a single cross on the side of each post where a beam will be housed. On the outside of each post, using a power saw and chisel, cut out and neaten a 140 x 45 mm housing just below the beam line to support the beam.

14 Plan for the beam to overhang the posts by 300 mm at either end.

Cut a stepped splay on the bottom edge. Cut the beam to length and shape it, removing any sharp edges by dressing with a hand plane. Place the beam in its housings and hold it in position with cramps. Drill holes through the beam and posts and secure them with two 12 mm diameter cup-head nuts and bolts.

FIXING THE RAFTERS

15 On each rafter, create a stepped splay and a 300 mm overhang to match those of the beam. Place the end rafters in line with the posts and space the two intermediate rafters evenly. Skew-nail each to the top of the beam with 75 x 3.75 mm galvanized lost-head nails.

FINISHING

16 Remove the temporary bracing and touch up the timber with your choice of paint or stain. This pergola is finished with two coats of white exterior acrylic paint.

17 Add a sheet of white-painted lattice to the roof, if desired.

11 Brace each post temporarily with timber off-cuts and, using a spirit level, recheck for vertical.

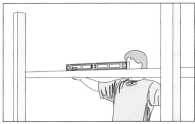

12 Using a spirit level and straight edge, transfer the position of the beam to the remaining three posts.

Shingle-roofed walkway

This small covered walkway, constructed from sawn oregon pine timber, is designed to mirror – and therefore complement – the general architectural style of a pre-existing two-storey house.

Here, special touches include panels of square lattice on the front and back and a gabled shingle roof.

The structure rests on individual concrete footings and is bolted in place with galvanized metal stirrups. Diagonal bracing with metal rods adds stability to the sides.

Follow the general construction advice provided for the flat-roofed freestanding walkway (see pages 158–63), then refer to the instructions on pages 148–57 for tips on designing and installing a gabled roof. Lay tiles and finish the roof with a length of metal ridge capping.

A shingle roof and coral and green paintwork echo the style of the house behind this walkway. Mounted on four concrete footings, this small pergola is finished with pairs of carved wooden brackets and a finial at the front.

Tools for building pergolas

Some of the most useful tools for constructing pergolas are shown below. Build up your tool kit gradually – most of the tools can be purchased from your local hardware or DIY store.

NAIL PUNCH Small metal tool used with a hammer for driving a nail head below the surface

ELECTRIC DRILL Power-driven drill with a variety of bits

SMOOTHING PLANE Used to smooth the surface of timber before sanding

CIRCULAR SAW Power saw for making straight cuts through timber, masonry or metal

MEASURING TAPE Spring-loaded, flexible steel blade marked in metric units of measure

JIGSAW Small electric saw with thin blade for cutting curves

G-CRAMP Holds work firmly to a surface

BUILDERS SQUARE Flat, right-angled device for determining 90 degree angles

CLAW HAMMER Hammer with a round head for driving nails and a split claw for removing them

SPIRIT LEVEL Used to test work for level (horizontal) and plumb (vertical)

ROUTER Used for hollowing out or cutting grooves in timber

CHISEL Used to cut grooves or housings in timber

POST-HOLE SHOVEL Two-handled spade for digging holes

Building barbecues

Types of barbecue

There are many different types of barbecue and several different types of fuel. Before you start building a barbecue, consider which types will best suit your home and lifestyle.

CHOOSING A BARBECUE

A built barbecue can become a feature in the garden landscape and an integral part of your outdoor lifestyle. It will, however, require considerable time and effort spent on construction, so be sure you will use it often enough to justify your work. You don't want to create a 'white elephant' that is never used. In some cases a portable or mobile unit may suit your lifestyle better.

Here are some points to consider:

• For any barbecue you will need a level site, preferably one close to the house, but for a built barbecue it will have to be large enough for the structure and for the cook and helpers to move safely around it.

• The area where you entertain may not be suited to a built barbecue (it may be a deck or tiled patio), and so you may have to settle for a portable or mobile unit.

• You will need to have time and basic bricklaying or stoneworking skills to build the barbecue, or be prepared to pay someone to do it.

• If you usually barbecue for only a couple of people, it may be a waste of fuel to use a large, built structure.

• Likewise, if you have many of your barbecues away from home (on picnics or holidays) you may find a portable barbecue more useful.

• You will probably find the cost of a built barbecue is similar to that of an equivalent mobile type.

BUILT BARBECUES

Built barbecues can be constructed for use with solid fuel or with a drop-in gas cooktop similar to those used in mobile barbecues. If you have plenty of wood on hand, fuel costs are nil. The costs of building a barbecue increase in proportion to the size and detail of the construction as well as with the choice of fuel.

PORTABLE AND MOBILE UNITS

Portable barbecues (those that can be packed up and put away or taken on picnics) and mobile barbecues (trolley types that can be moved to suit the weather or for storage) have become increasingly popular. They include electric barbecues, hibachi and kamado units, and kettle barbecues. However, these portable units are not very efficient when you are entertaining a large crowd and they often need to be stored or protected from the elements. They vary from simple types to elaborate

A built barbecue has the advantage that you can incorporate any number or size of preparation areas to suit your style of cooking and entertaining.

structures incorporating hoods, thermostats and side burners.

FUEL TYPES

Barbecues can be fired by a number of fuels. Those commonly used are solid fuels – such as wood, charcoal or briquettes – or gas or electricity.

SOLID FUELS

Solid fuels produce smoke, flames and smells that help create an 'outdoor' atmosphere. For some this is the essence of true barbecuing.

• Many people enjoy wood-fired barbecues for their traditional appeal, but you need time to collect the wood and kindling and get the fire going: wood is not a fuel for the cook in a hurry. Cooking is done over hot coals, so patience is needed as the flames heat the hotplate and then subside to provide a stable plate temperature. Using firelighters, which are cubes of compressed kerosene, makes it easier to start a fire as they burn longer than paper. The smoke generated by wood-fired barbecues can be a problem, especially if the wind is changeable. If you live in a smoke control zone, there may be restrictions on open fires, so check with your local authority. But wood is cheap and if there is an adequate supply available a wood-fired barbecue will give years of maintenance-free enjoyment.

• Charcoal is the residue of partially burnt wood. It fires quickly and provides ample heat for the barbecue. Lighting is easy if small pyramids of charcoal are built over a firelighter. Once alight, the charcoal can be spread out. It gives off little smoke and adds to the aroma. Charcoal is available at hardware stores.

• Briquettes are basically compressed charcoal and tend to burn longer. They can be lit in the same manner as charcoal although some brands have been soaked in kerosene and are easier to light. However, they do not lose the kerosene smell after lighting.

GAS

Gas is a clean and efficient form of heat supply, enabling accurate temperature control at the turn of a knob. Plate temperature is reached quickly and can be controlled throughout the cooking process. If you have mains gas supplied for heating and cooking, you may be able to have a line and connection made for the barbecue, but this must be done by a licensed gasfitter. It is more common to use a gas bottle, which gives you greater freedom in siting the barbecue. Do ensure you have an adequate supply of bottled gas before you start cooking, as there's nothing worse than running out when you are halfway through.

Reusable lava rocks (pieces of volcanic rock) are sometimes placed in a tray between the burner and the hotplate or grill to spread the heat.

ELECTRICITY

Like gas, electricity is clean, efficient and provides excellent temperature control. Electric barbecues for domestic use are, however, limited in size as plug-in household power supply has a maximum of 3000 watts. Electricity can, therefore, be used to fuel only small units.

SMOKING CHIPS

Smoking chips can be burnt with the barbecue to add flavour to the food being cooked. Popular flavours include hickory or mesquite.

A side bay has been constructed in this chimney for neat storage of the gas cylinder.

ADAPTING A CONVENTIONAL BARBECUE TO GAS

If you have a barbecue designed for solid fuel such as wood but find it is no longer practical, you can convert the existing firebox to accommodate a gas unit.

INSTALLING GAS BURNERS
BENEATH EXISTING HOTPLATE
1 Measure the width and depth of the firebox beneath the hotplate. Purchase a drop-in burner unit to fit. These units come in a frame with from two to five gas burners, each with its own control knob. The unit dimensions will vary with different makes, but the figures in the table below will act as a guide. You will also need to purchase a gas bottle, regulator and hose.

2 The recommended spacing between the burners and the hotplate is 75 mm. This ensures adequate flame contact and heating of the cooking area. There are various ways of supporting the burner framework so that it is at the correct height.

- Position bricks or concrete blocks at either side of the firebox and set the framework on them.
- Determine the correct height on the walls either side of the firebox and fix metal angle to the walls using expansion bolts.
- Position flat lintel or rods of steel at the correct height across the front and rear of the firebox.

INSTALLING COMPLETE NEW UNIT
Mobile gas barbecue units can be purchased without the trolley and placed into the firebox area. Measure the width and depth of the existing firebox and purchase a unit to fit. Remember that a unit with a roasting hood will need adequate space at the rear of the firebox so the hood can open fully.

As the unit will be exposed to all weather conditions, select one that has been finished completely in vitreous enamel or stainless steel. If possible, choose a unit with a cover that will protect the plate when the barbecue is not in use.

TYPICAL DROP-IN UNITS★

No. of burners	Length required	Depth required
2	430 mm	490 mm
3	610 mm	490 mm
4	760 mm	490 mm
5	960 mm	490 mm

★ Precise measurements will vary. Check before you purchase a unit.

Sandstone blocks are used to decorative effect for the corners of this elegant natural gas barbecue, while brick walls form the sides and a cross-wall to support the slab below the gas unit. Sandstone is also used for the top.

Designing a barbecue

A built barbecue becomes a permanent part of the garden. It is worthwhile spending time to plan it carefully so that you get the result you want.

FACTORS TO CONSIDER

If you have decided that a built barbecue will suit you best, you will now have to decide on a design. This will depend on how much space you have, the type of fuel, and whether you need preparation areas and storage for wood or gas bottles. You will also need to consider whether to include a chimney, either real or decorative, and any other structures such as seating, planter boxes, walls or pergolas. Finally, consider how much you can afford to spend.

MATERIALS

The materials that you choose for your barbecue will depend on the style of your home, the formality or informality of your garden design, your budget and, of course, the availability of the materials.

Brick barbecues are the most common because of their ease of construction and their ability to tie the house and garden landscape together. If the barbecue is sited close to the house and the house is brick, you will need to choose bricks that match it. If this is not necessary, you should select bricks that will be able to withstand the heat of the barbecue, particularly if it is wood-fired. Avoid the softer, calcium-silicate bricks and choose well-burnt, dry-pressed bricks if possible. Your local brick supplier will be able to advise you.

Stone barbecues are also popular in areas where York stone, limestone and sandstone can be easily purchased. York stone lends itself to a natural, rustic setting and is an ideal choice for wood-fired, informal designs. Choose carefully, however, as some stones such as limestone can 'explode' when subjected to great heat. Sandstone is a softer, more porous stone and allows for shaping and facing. This makes it a popular choice in more formal and traditional settings. It can be purchased in regular geometric shapes in either block or slab form. Sandstone is also available in split, irregular forms.

DIMENSIONS

The dimensions to be considered include not only the overall length, width and height of the unit, but also those of the surface areas that will be used for cooking and preparation. You will also need to consider the space required for the firebox or gas unit, and storage for wood, gas bottles and other accessories.

BRICK MEASUREMENTS★

Number of bricks	Length (mm)	Height (mm)
1	215	75
2	440	150
3	665	225
4	890	300
5	1125	375
6	1350	450
7	1575	525
8	1800	600
9	2025	675
10	2250	750
11	2475	825
12	2700	900
13	2925	975
14	3150	1050
15	3275	1125

★ Including allowance for 10 mm joints. To include half a brick, add 112 mm to the length.

If you are working in brick or cut stone, design the barbecue to suit full brick or block dimensions. This will make laying easier and you will avoid unnecessary cutting. Brick sizes vary quite considerably, but a standard brick size is 215 mm long x 100 mm wide x 65 mm high. The table above gives the numbers of bricks necessary for making up various lengths or heights. If your bricks are a different size, adjust the measurements to suit.

HOTPLATE

The size of the area required for cooking depends on the number of people to be fed. An average sized cooking plate of 930 x 600 mm caters for 12–15 people. If you usually cook for smaller numbers, reduce the plate size to 690 x 600 mm and then if you occasionally need extra space, you can bring out or hire a portable barbecue to supplement it.

When deciding on a plate size, ensure it will suit the brickwork dimensions. The two plate sizes given here will fit inside standard brickwork with a 10 mm gap all round for expansion. The plate can be cut to any size needed.

The steel plate should not be too thin or it will buckle over time. A good thickness is 6–8 mm. If the barbecue plate is larger than normal, increase the thickness or have steel rods welded on to the underside to prevent it bending or buckling.

PREPARATION AREA

Whether or not you incorporate preparation areas in the built unit, you will need to allow somewhere to place food and utensils during cooking. Most barbecue designs include a preparation area next to the hotplate on one or both sides. The size of this area can vary according to your needs and the space available. If the area is going to be used to store and prepare food before cooking as well as to serve guests, an area twice the size of the hotplate would be useful. If your barbecue setting includes a table where the cooked food, salads and utensils can be served, then a smaller preparation area would suffice.

When designing the preparation area, include an appropriate finish so that it will be easy to clean. Surfaces such as concrete and stone attract dirt and grease over time and would be better finished with wipe-clean surfaces such as ceramic tiles, sealed terracotta or slate.

WORKING HEIGHT

You should also consider the height of the preparation and cooking areas to avoid discomfort while cooking. An average height is between 850 and 950 mm, but if the main cook is particularly tall or short, you should adjust the height to suit. Eleven courses of brickwork will give a height of 825 mm while thirteen courses will give 975 mm.

STORAGE

Including preparation areas in your design often creates space for storage below. These storage areas can be left open to the weather or closed with doors. Shelves can be installed for utensils or equipment, or the space can be used to store wood or gas bottles. By providing covered storage for wood, you will ensure a dry supply of fuel in all weathers.

With gas-fired units, it is safer to store the gas bottle away from the burners and out of the weather. A small opening can be left in the brick jointing during construction so that

the gas line can be connected to the burners. Incorporate this into your planning and design stage or drill out a hole later. If doors are to be added to these areas, allow adequate ventilation in case of gas leakage. A gap at the top and bottom will allow air to circulate while protecting the area from the weather.

These areas are ideal for storing such things as the barbecue tools, perhaps hung on hooks on the backs of the doors, cleaning materials for the preparation areas, lava rocks or charcoal, smoking chips, dry matches, an ignition gun or even small garden tools and implements.

LOCATION

Deciding where to locate your barbecue can often be the most difficult part of building it. To get full use from your barbecue you need to locate it somewhere that is comfortable and convenient for cooking and entertaining.

Build the barbecue close to the house where you will have easy access to food, drinks and utensils. If you have an outdoor living area, perhaps with a pergola or patio, it will naturally form part of that. A barbecue placed apart from the living area isolates the cook from the guests and is less likely to be used. If you have to build the barbecue any distance from the house, plan paths or walkways to link them.

The choice of location will also be influenced by the prevailing weather conditions, as using the barbecue will be more comfortable if it is not exposed to strong winds, direct sunlight or excessive shade. You may also require some privacy from your neighbours. If you are planning a structure in the grounds of a listed building, check with your local council before beginning work.

You may find it helpful to sketch a plan of your house and backyard on paper (preferably to scale). On a separate piece of paper draw your proposed barbecue area to scale and cut it out. This cut-out can then be moved around the backyard plan until you find the best location.

SURROUNDING AREA

Any outdoor entertainment area, whether large or small, needs to be level, hard-wearing and without drainage problems. If you have a sloping site, consider terracing or constructing a deck.

The size of the overall barbecue area will be determined by the amount of space available, the number of people you want to accommodate and your budget, but you should always include enough room for the cook to work unhindered and for the guests to be served comfortably.

If you don't plan to have a barbecue very often and don't intend to have large parties, a small paved area or deck may be sufficient. On the other hand, if you plan to use the barbecue for large-scale entertaining, it may be worthwhile creating a more elaborate area with roofing,

lighting, storage and preparation areas, seating and screening.

SURFACE MATERIAL

Select the surfacing material for the area carefully to provide an easy-care, comfortable and durable surround for the barbecue. Your choice will depend on the style of the house and landscaping, and your choice of material for the barbecue itself. For example, a barbecue constructed of sandstone blocks will often look best when it is surrounded by matching sandstone flagging.

Popular materials for surfacing the area around a barbecue include:
- brick pavers of clay or concrete
- house bricks
- concrete (either plain, stencilled or stamped)
- exposed aggregate
- slate
- tiles (terracotta or concrete)
- sandstone
- timber decking

If you use terracotta or slate, be aware that they provide a non-slip surface only if they are unsealed, but they are then likely to absorb grease from the barbecue.

Sandstone is porous and will show stains and discolour over time. It can be sealed, but you will need to check the manufacturer's instructions on a variety of sealants to select the best one for your paving.

Lawn is not a good choice for a barbecue surround as it tends to wear and remain wet underfoot. Loose materials such as gravel should also be avoided as they can be unstable. This is a decided disadvantage when you are carrying plates of food.

SHELTER

The barbecue area may need some protection from the weather, and the amount will depend on how exposed it is to wind and sun.

When looking at alternatives, consider the probable cost, ease of construction (and your level of skill) and how each will complement your existing house and garden landscape. The most important consideration is to create a functional, and yet comfortable, outdoor area.

Some possible structures are:
• roofing attached to the house;
• a separate cabana-type structure;
• a pergola or other open-timber framework which can be covered with light material such as lattice, canvas, overlapping fibreglass or metal sheeting;
• a trellis structure, perhaps used with a pergola to support climbing plants such as clematis;
• a screen or hedge of plants.

There are also less permanent means of shelter such as umbrellas. You may also be able to take advantage of existing shelter such as trees, parts of the building, fences or walls, thus reducing your costs.

LIGHTING

If you plan to use the barbecue area in the evenings you will need adequate lighting. Family and friends will want to see what they are eating,

and the cook will need to see what is being cooked. At the barbecue itself, a light directly overhead or directed on to the cooking area from the side is best. Fluorescent lighting casts fewer shadows, but an overhead spot on to the cooking and preparation surfaces will suffice.

Within the barbecue area, more subtle lighting can be used to create atmosphere and to highlight garden or landscaping features. Fixed permanent lighting must be installed by a qualified electrician, or you may choose to use moveable garden lighting or portable floods, which can be run from a nearby power source.

Whatever you choose, it is important to decide about lighting during the planning stage so that electrical conduits can be run beneath any paving or concrete.

COSTS

The costs involved in the construction of a barbecue area depend on how elaborate it is. You will probably find that the cost of the barbecue itself will be minimal within the overall project budget.

Some of the features to include in your costing are:
• the barbecue itself
• retaining walls or screens
• paving or other surfacing
• any shade structure
• seating
• a lighting and power supply

Neat, accurate bricklaying is essential if you are to have a barbecue that looks attractive as well as adds to the amenities of your home.

Brickwork basics

Most built barbecues are constructed from bricks. Basic bricklaying is not difficult but it does require some practice to achieve a neat result.

SETTING OUT THE SLAB

1 Mark out the area for the concrete slab, ensuring the corners are at 90 degrees. Check them with a builders square or use the 3-4-5 method (see the box on page 180). When the area has been laid out, check the corners are at right angles by measuring the two diagonals: if they are the same length, then the area has been correctly laid out.

2 Excavate the area to a depth of 100 mm, removing grass and any other vegetation.

3 Form up the perimeter with timber formwork that will hold the concrete in position until it has hardened. For the formwork use long, straight pieces of timber held in place with a few pegs around the outside. Check the formwork is square and level before fixing it in position with nails and more pegs. Build in a slight crossfall to make it easier to hose down the slab once it is in use.

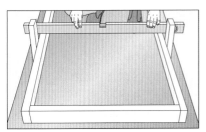

3 Form up the perimeter with timber formwork and check it for square and level before fixing it in position.

TOOLS FOR BRICKLAYING

- Measuring tape
- String line
- Spirit level
- Builders square
- Spade
- Hammer
- Steel mesh cutters or angle grinder
- Shovel
- Wheelbarrow
- Wooden float
- 75 mm edger
- Coloured china pencil
- Mortar board
- Bricklaying trowel
- Gauge rods (if needed)
- Corner blocks
- Club hammer and bolster
- Scutch hammer
- Jointing tool (optional)
- Small brush
- Sponge and bucket

THE 3-4-5 METHOD

From the corner point measure down one side 300 mm and down the other 400 mm (or you can use any multiples of these numbers, for example, 3 m and 4 m or 600 mm and 800 mm). The hypotenuse (or diagonal) should equal 500 mm (or the appropriate multiple) if you have made a right-angle triangle.

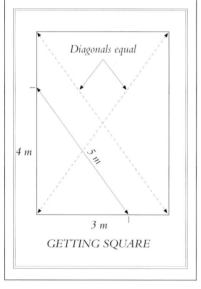

GETTING SQUARE

4 Fit a sheet of steel reinforcing mesh inside the formwork, ensuring a 50 mm clearance around the edges.

4 Lay a sheet of steel reinforcing mesh inside the formwork, making sure there is a 50 mm clearance around the edges. The mesh will increase the strength of the concrete and prevent it cracking at a later time. Support the mesh on mesh men to lift it to the centre of the slab.

THE CONCRETE

5 Prepare the concrete.

• If you are hand mixing the concrete, a mix of four parts coarse aggregate (gravel), two parts fine aggregate (sand) and one part cement (4:2:1) is sufficient. You will probably find 10 mm sized aggregate easiest to work. Mix these dry materials together with a shovel, form a well in the centre and then pour enough water into the well to achieve an even consistency.

• Ready-mixed concrete is delivered in quantities that increase by 0.2 m^3. The required product standard is Gen 3 or ST4, each with a minimum amount of 20 kg cement per metre.

6 Pour the concrete into the formwork, using a spade or shovel to

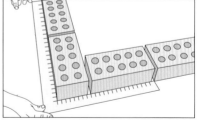

10 Lay out the first course of brickwork and use a builders square to check the corners are at 90 degrees.

spread it out. Keep the concrete level as you go and make sure that it is packed firmly under the steel reinforcing mesh.

7 Screed the concrete off by moving a piece of timber in a sawing motion across the top of the formwork. Use a hammer to tap along the side edge of the formwork to help settle the concrete edge and to prevent honeycombing (air pockets).

8 Use a wooden float to cream up the surface and pack the concrete at the edges hard. Then use an edger to roughly edge the slab and push the stones down.

9 Allow the concrete to dry to a point where only the surface is still workable. Refinish the surface and edge. Allow the concrete to cure, keeping it damp, for 2–3 days.

THE BRICKWORK

10 Using a straight edge as a guide, lay out the first course of brickwork. Allow for 10 mm joints between the bricks. Use a builders square to

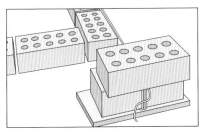

11 Set taut string lines along the bricks, allowing an extra 10 mm in height for the bed of mortar.

CONSTRUCTING A GAUGE ROD

Construct a gauge rod by placing a length of timber vertically against an existing 'quality' brick wall. Mark on the timber the location of the top of each brick course for the number of courses needed for your barbecue. Use a square to draw each mark around all sides of the gauge rod.

Alternatively, look at the height dimensions of brickwork provided on page 174 and transfer these on to the gauge rod.

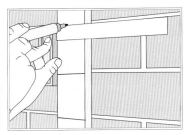

Mark on the timber the location of the top of each brick for the number of courses needed.

check the corners are at 90 degrees and measure the internal diagonal distance from corner to corner. The measurement should be the same both ways. Use a masonry pencil to mark the concrete along both sides of the brickwork, making guidelines to use later when laying the bricks.

11 Set taut string lines, allowing an extra 10 mm in height for the bed of mortar. Remove the bricks.

12 Unless you are an experienced bricklayer, construct gauge rods (see the box on page 181). Stand them vertically at each corner of the layout, fixing them in position with braces and pegs. Use a spirit level to make sure they are vertical both ways. As you work upwards, attach a string line for each course at the indicated mark.

13 Prepare a mortar mix. As bricks in a barbecue are affected by variations in temperature and should be able to expand and contract, use a mix ratio that is not too strong. Six parts sand, one part cement and one part lime (6:1:1) is ideal. You can also add a plasticizer to make the mix more workable. Mix the dry materials together thoroughly, perhaps in a wheelbarrow, and then add enough water to make a pliable mix with a consistency a bit like toothpaste. Mortar is useful for only about one and a half hours, so don't mix too much at once.

14 Transfer the mortar to a mortar board. To keep it soft and pliable you will have to continually work it backwards and forwards across the board with a trowel.

15 Spread the mix between the guidelines and lay the first course of bricks to the set string lines. On the trowel, pick up enough mortar to lay two bricks. Spread it on the slab (or existing brick course) at an even thickness of 15–20 mm. Pick up a brick, apply mortar to one end and position it on the bed of mortar, butting up to the last brick laid. Use the trowel to tap the brick into place so that the joints are a consistent thickness of 10 mm and then remove excess mortar. Check that the course is level with a spirit level and adjust by tamping if necessary.

16 Always lay the corners first and then fill in the wall between them. Lay the bricks so that the joints are staggered. To do this you will need to cut some bricks in half. Place a bolster at the appropriate place on the brick and hit it firmly with a club hammer. A scutch hammer can be used to chip off small pieces.

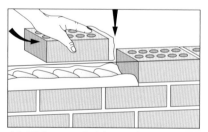

15 *Pick up a brick, apply mortar to one end and place it on the bed of mortar, against the last brick laid.*

17 *As you build, use the spirit level to check that the walls are vertical and the courses are aligned.*

MAKING A GOOD FIRE

If you are going to use solid fuel in your barbecue you need to plan the firebox carefully to ensure you have a fire that burns well.

Fire needs fuel and oxygen and the secret of a good fire is to get plenty of air to it. If the fuel is set on a grate, air can be drawn up from underneath and then into the flue and up the chimney. A chimney helps produce a good draught, which is why one is often incorporated into a barbecue.

The fire will stop burning when it runs out of fuel or when the air supply is cut off. Having some method of controlling the air supply, therefore, gives you greater control over the fire. In the Barbecue with two fires on page 190 dampers are set into the chimney to control the air flow.

The opening to the flue should be two or three courses high, and the top should be level with the hotplate so that smoke is drawn up the chimney. If the opening is too small, smoke will build up and then flow out of the front of the barbecue – right into the cook's face!

A metal damper serves to open and close off each half of the chimney in this barbecue (page 190).

17 As you build, use the spirit level to check that the walls are vertical and the steps are aligned.

18 To tie spur walls into the main wall, cut a notch halfway across and along the brick for the main wall and remove one-quarter of a brick for the spur wall. (Or use brick ties.)

19 Clean excess mortar off the bricks before it dries. Next day, wash the wall with water and a stiff brush. If necessary, wait several days and use a solution of 1 part hydrochloric acid

to 20 parts water to clean the brickwork. Always add the acid to the water (never water to acid), and wear protective goggles and gloves.

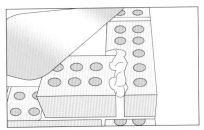

18 To join walls, cut a notch in the brick for one wall and remove one-quarter of a brick for the other wall.

Barbecue with rear screen

This gas-fired barbecue has a fake chimney, which forms part of an in-built screen that divides the barbecue from a covered eating area directly behind it and helps support a deck.

DESIGN

This barbecue unit of dry pressed brick with raked joints has a drop-in gas unit with grill and hotplate. The unit has five gas burners. On either side of the cooking area is a 525 x 920 mm preparation area covered with tiles, with storage areas for gas bottles and other equipment below.

The chimney is not functional as it does not open into the firebox, and it has been included for decorative

The back wall of this barbecue effectively divides open and covered entertaining areas but could also be used to screen off an unsightly view.

effect. It forms part of a rear screen with decorative metal grilles. In the photograph below the screen helps support a deck, which provides cover for a sunken eating area, but an extra two or three courses could be added to the top instead to make it suitable for any location.

BRICKLAYING

1 Set out and lay the 3000 x 700 mm area for the slab following the instructions on pages 179–81.

2 Following the bricklaying instructions on pages 181–3 and the

set-out diagram for this barbecue on page 186, build the end corners and end arms to a height of ten courses. Stretch a taut string line between the corners to use as a guide when laying the rest of the back wall. Keep an eye on the perpendicular joints, making sure that they stay straight. On the tenth course of the end arms lay only the outside row of bricks.

3 Complete the back wall, the two centre arms and the front wall up to the sixth course. Tie the fourth course of the centre arms into the back wall as shown on page 183.

4 Continue the brickwork, laying the back wall and the two centre arms to the ninth course, leaving the front wall open. Tie the arms to the back wall in the eighth course. Then lay the tenth course, but lay only the

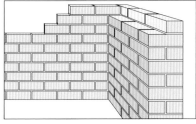

2 Build the end corners and end arms to ten courses, but on the tenth course of the arms lay only the outside row.

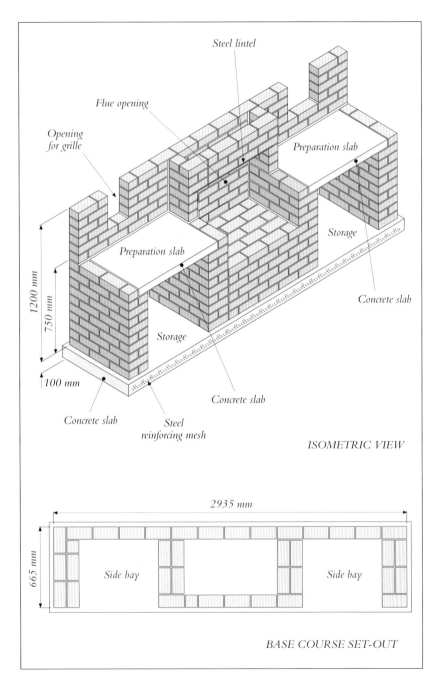

Steel lintel

Flue opening

Opening
for grille

Preparation slab

Preparation slab

Storage

Concrete slab

1200 mm

750 mm

Storage

100 mm

Concrete slab

Steel
reinforcing mesh

Concrete slab

ISOMETRIC VIEW

2935 mm

665 mm

Side bay

Side bay

BASE COURSE SET-OUT

MATERIALS★

- Concrete for ground slab: 0.25 m³ ready-mixed (extra 0.2 m³ if footing required for back wall), *or* cement, sand and 10 mm aggregate
- 100 x 50 mm timber for formwork
- Ten timber pegs
- A142M steel reinforcing mesh: 3200 x 700 mm and two 850 x 500 mm
- Cement, bricklayers sand, lime and plasticizer for mortar
- 427 full bricks and 32 half bricks (for sixteen courses)
- 90 x 8 mm steel lintel 960 mm long

- Two aluminium decorative grilles
- Tiles 1.6 m³
- 75 x 3.5 mm galvanized round-head nails
- Two 940 x 600 mm sheets fibre cement or marine plywood
- Concrete for preparation slabs: 0.12 m³
- Sand to fill firebox cavity
- Five-burner gas unit to fit
- Gas bottle with regulator and hose
- Timber 75 x 38 mm and 2935 mm long *or* two 90 x 8 mm lintels 400 mm long

★ Finished size: 2935 x 665 mm and 1200 mm high (based on a brick size of 215 x 100 x 65 mm).

inside row on the arms so as to make ledges. These ledges will support the concrete preparation slabs above the storage areas.

5 The chimney is built on the inside rows of the centre arms and its walls are only one brick thick. It projects in one brick length from the back wall. Lay the first two courses of the chimney sides as you build up the back wall by another two courses to form the screen. Mark the positions of the grilles on the top of the bricks and leave space for them as you build higher (the grilles in this unit were one and a half bricks long and four bricks high).

6 Lay another course on the back wall and chimney sides and then place a 90 x 8 mm bar lintel in

4 On the tenth course lay only the inside row on the centre arms to make ledges for the concrete pads.

6 Place a lintel in position over the firebox and continue laying courses for the chimney and back wall.

HINT

Instead of a complete gas unit, this barbecue would work well with a hotplate and five-burner gas framework. Insert two 10 mm diameter rods across the firebox before laying the tenth course and rest a 12 mm thick hotplate on them. The gas burners are placed under the hotplate, supported on either side by concrete blocks or a couple of bricks.

position over the sides of the chimney to support the upper part of the chimney. Complete another three courses of brickwork (or more if you want the chimney and screen taller; if so, use 400 mm long lintels over the grille openings).

TO FINISH

7 Paint the grilles the desired colour. Each grille rests on two points which are recessed into the brickwork to hold the grilles in place. Drill two holes 10 mm deep into the bricks with a 10 mm masonry bit. Stand the grille in position. Fix a timber plate across the top of the back wall.

8 Fill the firebox cavity with sand, finishing 70 mm below the finished height to allow bricks to be placed on it. Tamp and lightly hose the sand to compact it. Screed the sand to provide a level surface. Lay the bricks over the area in a stretcher pattern and compact them with a piece of

timber and a club hammer. Grout the joints with fine sand.

9 Form the concrete slabs for the preparation areas by placing a sheet of fibre cement or plywood on top of each side bay. Nail a 1 m length of 100 x 50 mm timber to the face of the board to contain the concrete and brace the centre of this cross-piece to support the weight of the concrete. Place an 850 x 500 mm sheet of steel mesh in the centre of the slab to prevent cracking. Mix and pour the concrete (see pages 180–1) and finish the slabs with the wooden float. Allow to cure for 2–3 days.

10 Fix tiles to the concrete surface to make an easy-to-clean surface (see the box opposite).

11 The gas bottle is safest stored in one of the side storage areas away from the flames. If necessary, drill a 12 mm diameter hole through the brickwork for the gas line.

12 Position the gas unit, connect the gas and light the barbecue.

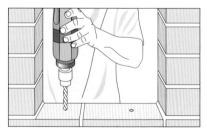

7 For the grilles drill two holes 10 mm deep into the brickwork with a 10 mm masonry bit.

LAYING CERAMIC TILES

1 Tiles are normally sold by the square metre, so calculate the amount you will need, including about 10 per cent extra to allow for breakage. The concrete base should be four weeks old before you start.

2 Ensure the surface to be tiled is completely clean. An ideal solution for cleaning concrete is one part hydrochloric acid to six parts water. Always add acid to water and wear goggles and gloves.

3 Lay out the tiles on the area to be covered. Adjust them to minimize the number of tiles that will have to be cut and so that the cut tiles are at the back or side edges of the area. Mark the cut on the back of the tile with a pencil, allowing for joints. Score along the line, place a nail under the line and snap down to break the tile.

4 Use a spatula to place the mortar or adhesive on the surface. A sand and cement mortar is fine, although prepared tiling adhesives are easier to use. With a notched trowel, spread mortar over 1 m² at a time. The trowel makes ridges that improve the grip on the tile.

5 Place the tiles in the mortar and settle them with a twist of the hand to remove air bubbles. Use nylon spacing crosses to achieve constant joint widths.

6 Gently clean off excess mortar before it dries, using a damp sponge and rinsing it frequently.

7 Leave the tiles for at least 24 hours and then apply grout with a rubber squeegee, working the grout well into the joints. Use a sponge to wipe off excess grout before it sets.

8 Wait 24 hours and then polish the surface of the tiles with a soft, dry cloth or crumpled newspaper.

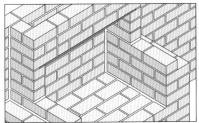

8 Fill the firebox cavity with sand, add a layer of bricks and compact them. Fill the joints with fine sand.

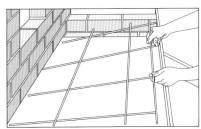

9 Nail a timber across the face of the preparation area to retain the concrete, and place steel mesh in the centre.

The chimney on this barbecue can draw smoke from one or both fires at the same time and has a directional cap to direct smoke away from the cooking area. A custom-made hinged stainless steel cover fits over the hotplate.

Barbecue with two fires

This barbecue is fuelled by two wood fires located at either end, so that the cook does not have to stand in front of the fire while cooking and can instead work at the large tiled area between the hotplate and chargrill plate. The unusual design does mean a little more work in construction.

- Bricklaying tools (see page 179)
- Angle grinder with masonry blade for cutting tiles

The chimney can draw smoke from either fire or from both at the same time. It is divided down the centre and has metal dampers that open and close the flues as required. A stainless steel cap sits on top of the chimney to direct smoke away from the cooking area.

A custom-made hinged stainless steel cover fits over the hotplate. This protects the plate when it is not in use, but can also be used when smoking or baking foods.

BRICKLAYING

1 Mark out the 2650 x 1250 mm area for the concrete slab and lay the concrete following the instructions on pages 179–81.

2 Follow the bricklaying instructions on pages 181–3 and the set-out diagram on page 193 to construct both ends of the front and back walls to a height of five courses.

3 Fill in the double brick walls to a height of five courses, at the same time building the dividing wall in the chimney and the two cross-walls. Make sure they are laid square to the front and back walls and that the chimney dividing wall is exactly in the centre of the chimney. Tie them in at least every fourth course by

DESIGN

This large unit is constructed of dry-pressed brick with flush jointing. It is fuelled by wood fires located at either end of the structure. One fire heats a large hotplate and the other a chargrill plate, allowing a choice of cooking styles, or two cooks can work at the one time to cater for a large group. The tiled preparation area is located between the hotplate and grill.

MATERIALS★

- Concrete for ground slab: 0.34 m³ ready-mixed, *or* cement, sand and 10 mm aggregate
- 100 x 50 mm timber for formwork
- Timber pegs and nails
- A142M steel reinforcing mesh: 2600 x 1200 mm, 500 x 585 mm and two 790 x 585 mm
- Tie wire and mesh men
- Cement, bricklayers sand, lime and plasticizer for mortar
- 630 bricks
- Two steel lintels 655 x 90 x 8 mm
- Four steel lintels 300 x 90 x 8 mm
- Steel lintel 1130 x 90 x 8 mm

- Steel lintel 435 x 90 x 8 mm
- 5 mm thick fibre cement sheeting: 525 x 665 mm and two pieces 890 x 665 mm
- Concrete for preparation and two firebox slabs: 0.18 m³
- Hotplate 865 x 525 x 12 mm
- Grill plate 420 x 525 mm
- Stainless steel hotplate cover
- Two steel flue dampers 345 x 115 x 5 mm with handles
- Stainless steel chimney cap
- 2.3 m² tiles
- Tile fixative
- Grout for tiles

★ Finished size: 2475 x 890 mm; height of cooking surface 810 mm, total height including chimney 1620 mm (based on brick dimensions of 215 x 100 x 65 mm).

---

notching out and overlapping the brickwork as shown in step 18 on page 183. When the mortar has set, position a 655 x 90 x 8 mm steel lintel on the fifth course at either end of the barbecue unit so that it sits across the opening.

4 Lay the sixth course right around the structure but at the ends where the firebox slabs will go use only a single skin of brickwork.

5 Once the brickwork has set, place a base of fibre cement sheeting over

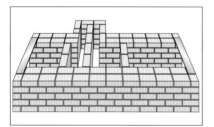

3 Fill in the double brick walls to five courses and position a steel lintel across the opening at each end.

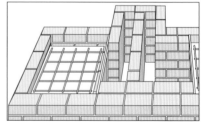

5 Set in place a base of fibre cement sheet and steel mesh ready to pour the concrete for the firebox slabs.

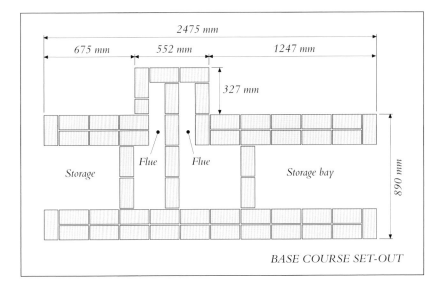

2475 mm

675 mm 552 mm 1247 mm

327 mm

Flue Flue

Storage

Storage bay

890 mm

BASE COURSE SET-OUT

the storage bays, with timber supports below. Add steel mesh. Mix concrete for the two firebox slabs as described on pages 180–1, finishing at the height of the sixth course. Leave the slabs to set.

6 Lay the 1130 x 90 x 8 mm lintel between the slabs and immediately behind the front double brick wall. This will support a third row of bricks under the central preparation

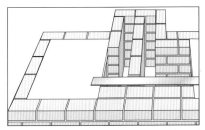

6 Lay the 1130 x 90 x 8 mm lintel between the slabs and immediately behind the front double brick wall.

area so as to narrow the flue and help to move smoke from the fires towards the chimney.

7 Lay the ends of the front and rear walls to nine courses, at the same time laying bricks for the seventh course across the ends over the lintels but leaving the eighth and ninth courses open for the firebox openings (see diagram on page 195). Set string lines off the ends and fill in the middle of the walls, including the chimney and chimney dividing wall.

8 Place two 300 x 90 x 8 mm lintels side by side over the firebox opening at each end. Place a 435 x 90 x 8 mm lintel across the two flue openings so the tenth course of the rear wall can continue straight across. Lay the tenth course around the outside in single brick only, as this

will contain the concrete slab. Allow the brickwork to set.

9 Place a 890 x 665 mm piece of fibre cement sheeting on top of the ninth course of brickwork where the central slab will go. Using 100 x 50 mm timber, form up the two sides to contain the concrete at the edge of the hotplate and grill areas. Place a piece of steel mesh inside the formwork. Cover this area with concrete to the height of the tenth course. Allow it to set before removing the formwork.

10 Continue the chimney to the height of twenty courses, using gauge rods as in step 12 on page 182. Construct the rib in the centre using bricks laid on edge so that each half of the chimney is exactly 135 mm wide. Tie the rib to the outer chimney walls every third course by notching bricks or using metal brick ties. On the front face omit the mortar between courses 17 and 18 to exactly the width of the inside openings. This is to allow the metal dampers to slide in and out, opening

and closing each flue as required and controlling the burn rate of each fire.

TO FINISH

11 The width available for the hotplate and grill is 665 mm. If your hotplate and grill are narrower, you can make the opening narrower by cutting bricks and mortaring them inside the edge bricks of the hotplate and grill areas. The width of the top surface around the hotplate and grill can also be varied to suit the tiles you are using.

12 Tile the surface of the brickwork and concrete preparation slab (see the box on page 189).

13 Place the hotplate and chargrill on the supporting brickwork. The optional stainless steel chimney cap and hotplate cover can be made at most metal fabrication or engineering shops. Fix the cap with four screws into plastic plugs.

14 Before using the barbecue, fire up both ends, open the flues and check the chimney works correctly.

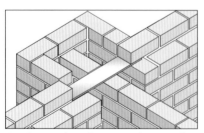

8 Place a lintel across the two flue openings so the tenth course of the rear wall can continue straight across.

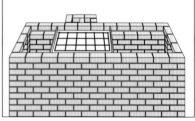

9 For the preparation slab, place fibre cement on top of the ninth course, form up the two sides and add mesh.

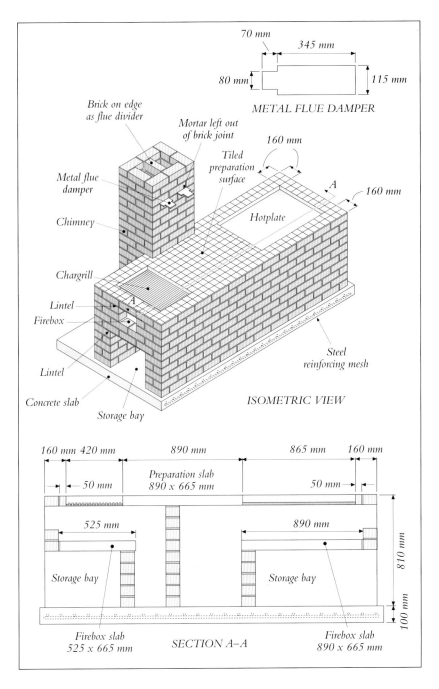

70 mm

345 mm

80 mm

115 mm

METAL FLUE DAMPER

Brick on edge
as flue divider

Mortar left out
of brick joint

Tiled
preparation
surface

160 mm

A

160 mm

Metal flue
damper

Hotplate

Chimney

Chargrill

Lintel

A

Firebox

Steel
reinforcing mesh

Lintel

Concrete slab

ISOMETRIC VIEW

Storage bay

160 mm 420 mm

890 mm

865 mm

160 mm

50 mm

Preparation slab
890 x 665 mm

50 mm

525 mm

890 mm

810 mm

Storage bay

Storage bay

100 mm

Firebox slab
525 x 665 mm

SECTION A–A

Firebox slab
890 x 665 mm

On either side of this barbecue a brick wall with two arms supports a slatted seat that can double as a preparation area. The surrounding area is surfaced with clay pavers laid in a herringbone pattern.

Barbecue with decorative chimney

This neat gas-fired barbecue incorporates a non-functional chimney but requires only basic bricklaying skills. The storage area is topped with slate and closed with timber doors.

MATERIALS★

- Concrete for slab: 0.2 m³ ready-mixed, *or* cement, sand and 10 mm aggregate
- 100 x 50 mm timber for formwork
- Timber pegs and nails
- A142M steel reinforcing mesh: 1500 x 700 mm
- Tie wire
- Cement, bricklayers sand, lime and plasticizer for mortar
- 400 bricks (extruded bricks were used for the barbecue shown opposite)

- 25 paving bricks
- Flat steel lintel 1100 x 90 x 8 mm
- Flat steel lintel 445 x 90 x 8 mm
- Five pieces of slate 217 x 100 mm
- Stainless steel cover lid
- Five-burner gas unit
- Natural gas fuel line, stopcock and pressure regulator
- Two 420 mm lengths of steel angle to support gas unit
- Four 50 mm expansion bolts

★ Finished size: 1462 x 665 mm without chimney; height of arms 1050 mm; chimney 552 x 327 mm and 2100 mm high (based on brick measurements of 215 x 100 x 65 mm). For door materials see page 200.

The design

This barbecue is built with extruded bricks and ironed joints to accommodate gas burners that are fuelled by natural gas. There is a non-functional chimney, included for decorative effect, and a storage space below the cooking area is closed with double timber doors. The firebox is paved with slate. A custom-made stainless steel cover is placed over the gas burners when they are not in use.

TOOLS

- Bricklaying tools (see page 179)
- Circular saw
- Drill and drill bits
- Screwdriver
- Cork sanding block
- Router (optional)
- Chisels
- Tenon saw
- Sash cramps

BRICKLAYING

1 Mark out and prepare the 1560 x 750 mm area for the concrete slab and the 575 x 375 mm slab area for the chimney (see pages 178–81).

2 Following the bricklaying instructions on pages 181–3 and the set-out diagram opposite, lay three courses, which includes the front, sides, back and chimney, tying in the chimney at the third course (and every third course hereafter).

3 Lay the next six courses for the sides, back and chimney, but not the front as you need to create the opening for the storage area. At the end of the ninth course, place the 1100 mm lintel across the opening at the front to create a header above the doorway. Lay course number ten, including across the front.

4 Lay the next three courses, but again leave the front open to create the firebox.

5 Construct the remaining fifteen courses of the chimney. To create a flue opening, leave out courses 14 and 15 at the front of the chimney and place the 445 mm lintel across the opening. You will find it easier to lay the upper courses of the chimney if you brace two gauge rods in place and follow them rather than string lines. Constantly check with a spirit level as you work to make sure that the chimney is vertical.

6 To cap the holes in the top of the extruded bricks, use brick pavers as the final course on the unit. Alternatively, you can fill the holes with mortar or cover them with tiles or slate.

7 Using expansion bolts, fix a 420 mm length of steel angle to each side of the firebox to support the gas unit. The precise positioning of the angle will depend on the size of your gas unit. In this barbecue the angle was positioned 230 mm below the bottom of the flue opening and waterproof adhesive was used to glue paving bricks on to each piece of steel angle, to provide extra support for the gas unit.

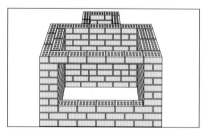

3 At the end of the ninth course, place a lintel across the opening and lay course number ten.

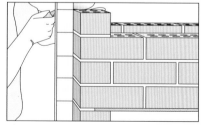

5 Construct the remaining fifteen courses of the chimney using two gauge rods as a guide.

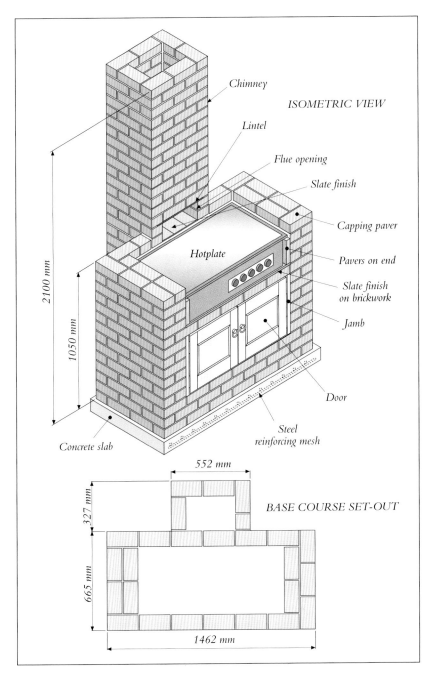

Chimney

ISOMETRIC VIEW

Lintel

Flue opening

Slate finish

Capping paver

Hotplate

Pavers on end

Slate finish
on brickwork

Jamb

2100 mm

1050 mm

Door

Steel
reinforcing mesh

Concrete slab

552 mm

327 mm

BASE COURSE SET-OUT

665 mm

1462 mm

MATERIALS FOR DOORS★

Part	Material	Length	Width	No.
Jamb	100 x 38 mm WRC	450 mm		2
Door stile	100 x 38 mm WRC	464 mm		4
Door rail	150 x 38 mm WRC	468 mm		4
Door panel	6 mm waterproof plywood	223 mm	305 mm	2

OTHER: Epoxy adhesive; abrasive paper; 3 m of beading; four plastic wall plugs; 25 x 1 mm panel pins; 50 mm x 8 gauge screws; four hinges and screws; two latches and screws; two handles; finish of choice

★ Western red cedar (WRC) is used for all timber components. Timber sizes given are nominal (see box opposite). Adjust the lengths to suit your structure.

8 To cap the holes in the extruded bricks above the storage area and at the base of the flue, mortar pieces of slate in place.

ADDING THE DOORS
9 Cut the jambs to length and fix them to each side of the opening by drilling holes in the brickwork. Plug the holes with plastic wall plugs before fixing the jambs with screws.

10 Measure the width of the opening inside the frame and subtract 10 mm to allow a 3 mm gap between the doors and the jambs. Measure the height of the opening, subtract 6 mm to allow a 3 mm gap top and bottom. Divide the width by 2 to find the size of each door.

11 Cut four stiles 20 mm longer than the height. Cut two top and two bottom rails 20 mm longer than the width. Mark the overall height on the stiles.

12 Prepare mortise and tenon joints with tenons on the ends of the rails and mortises through the stiles inside the height marks. Cut them with a tenon saw and chisel. Glue the joints together with epoxy adhesive and hold them tight with sash cramps. Check them for square and adjust as required. Leave them to dry. Saw off the protruding tenon.

13 Sand the frame. Cut a 10 mm wide and 12 mm deep rebate around the inside face with a router, and square the corners with a chisel.

14 Cut and fit the door panels into the rebates. Cover the join on the outside face with beading. Nail it in position with 25 x 1 mm panel pins. Cut the stiles flush with the rails and plane the doors to fit (allowing a 3 mm clearance all round).

15 Fit hinges to each door. Fit handles and latches; attach the doors.

TO FINISH

16 Install the gas burner unit into the firebox area by sitting it on the paving bricks or directly on to the steel angle. Connect the gas and light the barbecue.

17 Make a protective stainless steel lid to cover the gas burners as well as the firebox area, or have one made to your specifications at an engineering, sheet metal or air-conditioning workshop. The cover should have a reasonable pitch so that water will run off it.

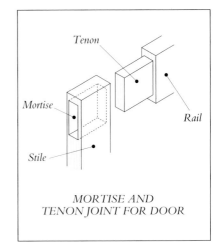

Tenon

Mortise

Rail

Stile

MORTISE AND TENON JOINT FOR DOOR

TIMBER

TIMBER CONDITIONS

Timber is sold in three conditions:
- sawn or rough sawn: brought to a specific (nominal) size by band saw
- planed: either planed all round (PAR), planed on two sides (P2S) or double planed (DP)
- milled: planed to a specific profile for architraves, skirting boards and so on

Planed timber is sold using the same nominal dimensions as sawn timber (e.g. 100 x 50 mm), but the surfaces have all been machined down to a flat, even width and thickness so that the '100 x 50 mm' timber becomes 91 x 41 mm when planed. The chart at right shows sizes for seasoned timber in its sawn (nominal) state and after dressing.

Milled timbers are ordered by their nominal sizes.

SAWN (NOMINAL) SIZE (mm)	SIZE AFTER DRESSING (mm)
25	19
31	23
38	30
50	41
75	66
100	91
125	115

TREATED TIMBER

Treated timber is sold in its finished size. Some available sizes are 70 x 35 mm; 70 x 45 mm; 90 x 45 mm.

TIMBER LENGTHS

Timber is sold in stock lengths, beginning at 1.8 m and increasing by 300 mm.

TIMBER FOR OUTDOOR USE

See pages 56–60 for details.

Originally designed for wood firing with metal plates for the hotplate and base of the firebox, this barbecue has been converted to natural gas.

Stone barbecue

This brilliant barbecue with central hotplate is built from shaped sandstone blocks. The construction is not difficult, but cutting the stones to shape is very time-consuming.

DESIGN

Although the curved design of this structure requires careful stone-cutting, the operation of the actual barbecue is simple. The central hotplate has an area of 930 x 700 mm, originally heated by a wood fire. Both the hotplate and plate for the firebox base are removable. A functioning chimney opens into the firebox immediately below the hotplate. The walls and chimney, which is tapered to reflect the curve of the wall, are constructed of rock-faced sandstone blocks that have been hand-cut and faced.

MATERIALS★

- Concrete for slab: 0.8 m³ ready-mixed, *or* cement, sand and 10 mm aggregate
- A142M reinforcing mesh: 7 m
- Tie wire and mesh men
- Two 100 x 50 mm straight timbers 3600 mm and 2000 mm long
- Timber formwork with pegs and nails for slab
- Sixty sandstone blocks 500 x 200 x 140 mm
- Plywood for block template

- Chinagraph pencil
- Ten sandstone cappers 500 x 380 x 50 mm and two 800 x 300 x 50 mm
- Off-white cement, white bricklayers sand, lime and plasticizer for mortar
- Steel plate 800 x 400 x 10 mm
- Steel rod 200 x 8 mm diameter
- Non-silicone water seal to protect stone
- Two steel plates 930 x 700 x 12 mm
- Copper pipe or expansion bolts

★ Finished size: 3320 mm wide and 1675 mm deep; chimney is 1470 mm high.

The barbecue has two curved wings, which enclose a court with sandstone flagging laid in a stretcher pattern. The ends of the two wings and the two centre walls are faced with blocks to give a buttress finish. The tops of these wings and the curved walls are capped with overhanging slabs of sandstone.

SETTING OUT

1 Lay the 3600 mm length of timber on the ground for the front of the barbecue. Drive in pegs either side of it to fix it in position. Hammer a 100 mm nail into the exact centre of the timber, so that it projects 50 mm.

2 In the 2000 mm length of timber drill a 5 mm diameter hole, 100 mm from one end. Locate and mark two positions 1300 and 1700 mm from the drill hole. At each mark hammer a 100 mm nail through the timber.

3 Place the hole over the centre nail of the fixed length of timber and rotate the 2000 mm timber in a semicircle so that the protruding nails scratch lines in the ground to indicate the front and back of the footings respectively. Leave the fixed board in position.

4 Excavate 300 mm deep trenches for the footings: the 400 mm wide curved wall plus 300 x 1100 mm at the back for the chimney and 700 x

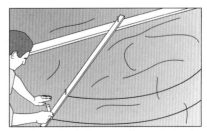

3 Place the hole over the nail in the fixed length of timber and rotate the shorter timber in a semicircle.

300 mm for each of the centre arms (see the diagram opposite). Lay the trench mesh. To bend the straight mesh around the curve, cut it in several places, kink it around the curve and re-tie it with tie wire. Fill the trenches with concrete and allow it to set for 2–3 days.

5 Take the nails out of the 2000 mm timber and mark two new locations at 1400 and 1600 mm from the drill hole. Once again, rotate the timber around the surface of the concrete, scribing two lines with a masonry pencil. Use these two curves as a guide when laying the blocks. Also mark guidelines for the centre walls and chimney. Adjust how far the curved arms project by moving the

fixed timber in as desired (in the barbecue on page 202 the timber was moved in 150 mm for a courtyard depth of 1250 mm). Again fix it firmly in place and leave it at least until the end blocks have been laid.

CUTTING THE STONE

6 Cut all the blocks for the curved wall to shape before you begin laying (see the box above). Begin by making a template of the required shape. Lay a 600 x 400 mm piece of plywood on the concrete footing over the drawn lines. Rotate the timber to scribe the curved lines on to the plywood. Again using the rotating timber, mark the lines for the ends of the blocks square to the curve and 500 mm apart, so that a complete block shape is created. Cut out the shape with a jigsaw.

7 Prepare a good solid bench (there should be no bounce) at a height that will allow you to stand up straight with an undressed stone beneath the stone being cut. Ensure the surface and blocks are clear of dust and grit.

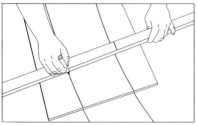

6 To cut the wall blocks, lay plywood on the footing and scribe the curved lines on to the plywood.

8 Place the template on top of a block of stone and mark the shape

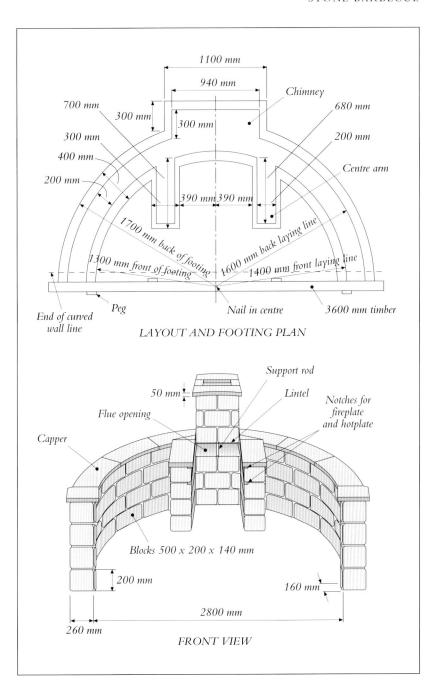

LAYOUT AND FOOTING PLAN

1100 mm
940 mm
Chimney
700 mm
300 mm
300 mm
680 mm
300 mm
200 mm
400 mm
200 mm
Centre arm
390 mm 390 mm
1700 mm back of footing
1600 mm back laying line
1300 mm front of footing
1400 mm front laying line
Peg
Nail in centre
3600 mm timber
End of curved wall line

FRONT VIEW

Support rod
Lintel
50 mm
Flue opening
Notches for fireplace and hotplate
Capper
Blocks 500 x 200 x 140 mm
200 mm
160 mm
2800 mm
260 mm

with a coloured chinagraph pencil. Using a power wet saw with a 300 mm diamond-tipped blade, cut along the two end lines.

9 Square two lines from the marked curves down each cut end of the block. Turn the block over and place the template so it is in line with the vertical end lines before marking around the template again. Use a club hammer and bolster to cut the curved faces. Turn the block over regularly and work back gradually to the marked lines. Remove the sharp edges with the carborundum stone as you go. Cut sufficient blocks to complete the curved wall. It takes a professional stonemason 40–50 minutes to complete each stone, so don't be surprised if you have to spend an hour or more cutting each block. This work must be done carefully and cannot be hurried.

LAYING THE STONE

10 Mix the mortar using white sand, lime and off-white cement, matching the colour of the stone as closely as possible. Use a plasticizer if you want to make the mortar more pliable (see step 13 on page 182).

11 Start laying the first course at one end by putting a bed of mortar on the footing inside the marked curve. Lay the blocks to the centre of the curve, making sure they are vertical and level. Tap each into the correct position with the handle end of a club hammer, a rubber mallet or a block of 50 x 50 mm hardwood.

12 Lay from the other end to the centre. This means that any cut blocks in each course will occur in the centre, which will eventually be hidden by the firebox and chimney. Complete the first three courses.

13 Repeat for the fourth course, but leave out the centre two blocks to form the flue opening and to tie in the chimney. Using a circular saw with a masonry blade, cut a notch (25 x 25 mm) along the top edge of the third course of the flue opening. This notch will support the firebox plate and provide a seal to protect the stone from the smoke and soot.

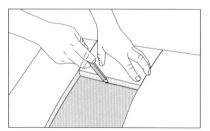

8 Place the plywood template on top of a block of stone and mark the shape with a coloured china pencil.

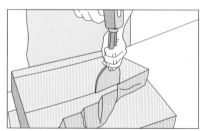

9 Use a club hammer and bolster to cut all the curved faces, working gradually back to the lines.

THE CHIMNEY

14 Cut the blocks for the chimney in the same way as those for the curved wall. The chimney tapers 105 mm from vertical on each side when measured from the base to the top (see the diagram at right). To achieve this, the outside end of the end blocks for each course tapers 15 mm. Set a sliding bevel at the appropriate angle to taper 15 mm for every 200 mm of block height. Using the bevel, mark a cutting line. Cut the blocks for the chimney and then dry-stack them to make sure that you are happy with the fit and the taper.

15 When you are satisfied, mortar the blocks for four courses in position. The first three courses butt against the curved wall, and the fourth is tied into it with two blocks.

16 Use the block template to mark the shape on the steel lintel and take it to a workshop that does oxy-acetylene cutting. Position the lintel on the overlapping blocks to create a flue opening and support the upper courses of the chimney. The lintel should be recessed 50 mm so that a ledge is left to support the hotplate.

17 Lay the remaining three courses of the chimney.

TO FINISH

18 Using the remaining stone blocks, construct the two straight arms in the centre. Butt the first two

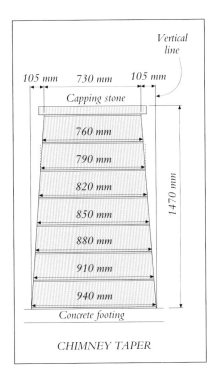

CHIMNEY TAPER

courses against the curved wall. Before laying the third course, cut a 25 x 25 mm notch from the inside top edge of each block as described in step 13. Repeat for the fourth course to accommodate the hotplate, and then lay the fourth course.

19 Lay the sixteen face blocks on the ends of the curved walls and centre arms. Those in the third and fourth courses of the arms are notched (50 x 25 mm) for the fireplate and hotplate. The face blocks are simply butted on. If you want to key them into the wall, drill 13 mm holes, which are then plugged with a 12 mm copper water pipe, or you can drill holes at a

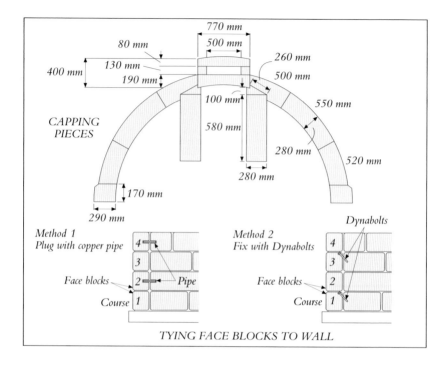

770 mm
500 mm
80 mm
130 mm
260 mm
400 mm
190 mm
500 mm
100 mm
550 mm

CAPPING
PIECES
580 mm

280 mm
520 mm
280 mm

170 mm
290 mm

Method 1
Plug with copper pipe

4
3
Face blocks
2 — Pipe
Course 1

Method 2
Fix with Dynabolts

Dynabolts
4
3
Face blocks
2
Course 1

TYING FACE BLOCKS TO WALL

45 degree angle and secure the blocks with 125 mm long expansion bolts. Place small timber wedges in the notched areas to prevent movement while the mortar is drying out.

20 Cut the capping pieces to cover the curved wall and centre arms. To

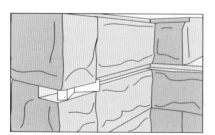

19 When laying the face blocks place wedges in the notched areas to prevent movement while the mortar is drying.

cut the curved pieces, make a template for the capping pieces as in step 6, but make the capping pieces 250 mm wide. The two chimney capping pieces are each cut from one solid piece of 800 x 300 mm stone, curved at front and back as for the curved wall blocks.

21 Because sandstone is porous, it is best to seal it before you use the barbecue in order to protect it from grease and smoke stains. Check the sealant manufacturer's directions and conditions of use before applying it.

22 Allow the mortar to set for at least two days, remove the wedges and insert the fireplate and hotplate.

STONE FOR OUTDOOR PROJECTS

Stone is one of the most attractive (although expensive) materials for outdoor projects. Strength and durability will vary according to each type of stone and the area from which it originally came.

SANDSTONE AND LIMESTONE

Sandstone and limestone can be brittle and soft, so for some projects you may prefer to choose harder, fine-grained stone such as granite or marble. However, sandstone is probably the most suitable stone for garden paving; it has a warm colour that mellows with age and it associates well with brick, timber, gravel and plants.

SLATE AND MARBLE

Among the harder, fine-grained varieties of stone is slate, which is a stylish, architectural material that can look particularly good when used in crisp, geometric designs. Like marble, it can take a high polish, but it is important to remember that it will become dangerously slippery in the rain. Slate also absorbs heat and can be hot to touch. As an edging it contrasts well with most other materials, from brick and timber to pale gravel. Marble is an extremely costly choice and is best used in formal situations. It will become very slippery when it is wet.

GRAVEL AND DECOMPOSED GRANITE

Loose fills, such as decomposed granite and gravel, are versatile and relatively cheap materials. They are very useful as a surface for curved and irregularly shaped outdoor areas. It is best to use them on level areas and to contain them with an edging. Larger granite or marble chips are also available. Gravel, which comes in different gauges and can range in colour from gold to grey, is ideal for paths and requires little preparatory work before being applied. Lay gravel on a hard base and compact it using a roller or other compacting tool.

GRANITE

Granite, a hard rock, is usually seen in the form of setts (which are small, irregular rectangles or squares laid in a pattern). Its uneven surface means it is not ideal for seating, but it does provide a firm grip when it is used on sloping sites.

COBBLES AND PEBBLES

Cobbles and pebbles are smooth, round stones ranging from 20 to 100 mm, which can either be laid loose or firmly bedded in mortar. You can use them to make intricate mosaic patterns. Bluestone, a very hard variety of stone, is usually found in the form of cobbles.

Tools for building barbecues

Some of the most useful tools for building barbecues are shown below. Build up your tool kit gradually – most of the tools can be purchased from your local hardware store.

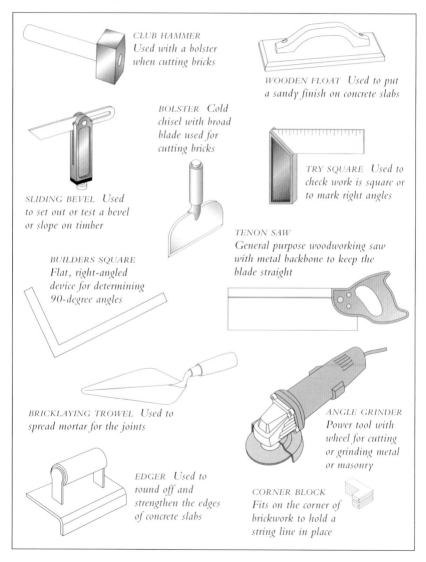

CLUB HAMMER Used with a bolster when cutting bricks

WOODEN FLOAT Used to put a sandy finish on concrete slabs

BOLSTER Cold chisel with broad blade used for cutting bricks

TRY SQUARE Used to check work is square or to mark right angles

SLIDING BEVEL Used to set out or test a bevel or slope on timber

TENON SAW General purpose woodworking saw with metal backbone to keep the blade straight

BUILDERS SQUARE Flat, right-angled device for determining 90-degree angles

BRICKLAYING TROWEL Used to spread mortar for the joints

ANGLE GRINDER Power tool with wheel for cutting or grinding metal or masonry

EDGER Used to round off and strengthen the edges of concrete slabs

CORNER BLOCK Fits on the corner of brickwork to hold a string line in place

Useful terms

baluster timber that supports a handrail

balustrade series of balusters supporting a handrail

barge capping metal weatherproof strip covering the gap between the roofing and the barge board

bearer timber that supports the floor joists

bevel surface that meets another at an angle other than 90 degrees

bird's-mouth housing notch cut in a rafter so that it sits over the wall plate

brace member, usually diagonal, used to keep a framework square

clearance hole hole equal to the diameter of a screw shank, enabling screw head to pull the joint tight

cleat small piece of timber used to connect two parts of a structure

collar tie horizontal member tying a pair of rafters together

countersink make a tapered recess so that a screw sits flush

dado mould decorative mould fitted around a post

face the surface from which measurements are made

fascia board board fixed to ends of joists to provide a neat finish

firebox the fire chamber or opening

flashing strip of impervious material fitted over a joint to prevent the entry of water

flue chimney shaft

footing concrete base for a post, pier or other superstructure

form box simple box used to hold wet concrete in place until it is set

header brick set through or across the wall

housing groove cut to form part of a joint

jamb side piece of doorway

joist timber to which flooring is fixed

ledger horizontal timber fixed to a wall to support cross-timbers

lintel horizontal support over an opening

mortise rectangular recess cut in timber to receive a tenon

PAR planned all round

pier column supporting the bearers and floor of a deck

pilot hole small hole to allow the thread of the screw to cut in and pull the joint tight

plumb vertical or perpendicular

post timber or steel vertical used to support the bearers and floor

profile pegs and batten to which stringlines are tied during set-out

rafter sloping member across the span between two points in the pergola (the ledger and the beam, the ledger and the ridge or the ridge and the beam) to support the roof

ridge capping metal strip formed over the ridge in order to provide a seal

riser vertical board under the tread of a stair

set-out measurements marked on the timber

shiplap interlocking panels

shoulder rise at side of joint where cut is made

skew nail or screw at an angle

span distance between two points of support (*see* rafter)

square a line draw a line at 90 degrees to the edge of the timber

stile vertical component of a frame

stirrup metal bracket fixed to the footing to support the post

straight edge any straight piece of timber used as a guide to make a straight line or cut

string one of a pair of diagonal timbers used to support the treads of a staircase

tenon projecting tongue on the end of a piece of timber that fits into a mortise

tread horizontal part of each step

trimmer timber cross-member fitted between two rafters

Index

Published by Murdoch Books UK Ltd
Ferry House, 51–57 Lacy Road, Putney,
London SW15 1PR

Murdoch Books® is a subsidiary of Murdoch Magazines Pty Ltd.

ISBN 1-85391-207-7

A catalogue record for this book is available from the British Library.

Managing Editor: Diana Hill

Editors: Catherine Magoffin, Rosalea Ryan, Sue Stravs

Design Concept: Marylouise Brammer

Designers: Norman Baptista, Michèle Chan, Michelle Cutler, Annette Fitzgerald,
Wing Ping Tong

Photography: Tony Lyon (pp. 6–49, 166–208), Andre Martin (pp. 106–67), Mil Truscott (pp.
50–106)

Stylists: Anna-Marie Bruechert (pp. 6–49), Louise Owens and Regina Walter (pp. 106–67),
Anne-Maree Unwin (pp. 166–208), Sophie Ward (pp. 50–106)

Illustrations: Stephen Pollitt

Authors: John Bowler (pp. 8–165) and Frank Gardner (pp. 166–209)

UK consultant: Ian Kearey

Production Manager: Lucy Byrne

CEO: Robert Oerton

Publisher: Catie Ziller

Group General Manager: Mark Smith

Do-It-Yourself Handbook *Outdoor Living Projects* has been compiled from the Mini
Workbooks *Garden Furniture*, *Building Decks*, *Building Pergolas* and *Building Barbecues*

Produced by Phoenix Offset. PRINTED IN CHINA. First published in the UK in 2001.

Publisher's Note: The information in this book has been compiled on the basis of
recommendations made and materials supplied by experts and/or by manufacturers of products.
The publisher accepts no responsibility for injury or loss resulting from application of any
technique or process contained in this book. Always follow the safety recommendations and
instruction manuals provided with tools and products.